Bicycling Magazine's
New Bike Owner's Guide

By the Editors of *Bicycling* Magazine

 Rodale Press, Emmaus, Pennsylvania

Printed in the United States of America on acid-free paper ∞

Compiled and edited by *Joe Kita*

Production editor: *Jane Sherman*
Copy editor: *Durrae Johanek*
Cover and interior design: *Lisa Farkas*
Cover photo: *Lori Adamski-Peek*

If you have any questions or comments concerning this book, please write:
    Rodale Press
    Book Reader Service
    33 East Minor Street
    Emmaus, PA 18098

Library of Congress Cataloging-in-Publication Data

Bicycling magazine's new bike owner's guide / by the editors of Bicycling
    magazine.
        p.   cm.
    ISBN 0-87857-872-2   paperback
    1. Cycling.   2. Bicycles.   I. Bicycling.   II. Title: New bike owner's
    guide.
    GV1041.B528   1990
    796.6−dc20   89-70310
                                                                        CIP

Distributed in the book trade by St. Martin's Press

2 4 6 8 10 9 7 5 3   paperback

CONTENTS

Introduction v

Part One: First Bike

   1 Choosing the Right Bike 1

   2 Questions to Ask Before You Buy 8

   3 Sizing a New Bike 9

   4 Clothing and Accessory Checklist 14

Part Two: First Miles

   5 The Principles of Pedaling 19

   6 Learning the Lingo 22

   7 Your First Riding Lesson 26

   8 Sharing the Road 29

   9 How to Out-Psych Hostile Drivers 31

  10 The Facts about Cycling Nutrition 33

  11 Fast Foods 35

  12 Perfect Your Riding Position 38

  13 Smart Shifting 47

  14 Basic Bike Care 53

  15 Fixing a Flat 57

Part Three: First Tour, First Century, First Race

  16 Setting Goals 62

  17 Training for an Extended Tour 65

  18 Preparing for a Century 69

19 Becoming a Racer 73
20 What Ails You? 85
21 75 Tips for Shaping Up, Losing Weight, and
     Riding Better 91

Part Four: First-Class Info
22 Questions and Answers 99
23 Where to Go for More Information 115

Credits 119

◳ INTRODUCTION

The new kid in school. That's how I feel as I step inside *Bicycling*'s bike shop. As the newest and most unlikely member of the magazine's staff, I've arrived for the first real bicycle ride of my adult life—an 18-mile jaunt with the other editors. The room is filled with bikes, the clickety-clack of cleats on cement, and several bona fide bikies pumping tires and tightening quick-releases. For me, it's a strange, somewhat unsettling scene.

I'm accustomed to tennis rackets, to the quiet echo of a basketball in a gym, the anticipatory excitement of lacing my running shoes. I've always considered myself a passable recreational athlete, but until today I've never been a cyclist. This ride is my initiation.

In the parking lot, everyone is wearing black cycling shorts and bright jerseys inscribed with such words as Campagnolo or Cinelli. I'm in gym shorts and an old T-shirt advertising Buckman's Car Wash. Somebody asks my shoe size. I say 11. He looks down at my tattered Reeboks and tells me I probably wear 45. Forty-five? Forty-five what? We start the ride.

The first miles are easy. Breezing by the autumn-tinted farmland, I feel as if I could ride forever. But a passing van scares me, and I steer off the road, just managing to keep my balance. After a few more miles my legs burn, my breathing deepens, and I discover genital numbness. Jeez, basketball was never like this. By the time I reach the trip's midpoint, it seems as if I *have* been riding forever.

It feels like the fifth set, the fourth period, the last lap—but I've only been riding 45 minutes. I'd always heard a good workout takes a lot more time on a bike, that you need to cycle three times as long to equal the fitness benefits of a run. I must have heard wrong.

Cycling, I found out, works the legs, butt, back, and most important, the heart. A 45-minute ride is comparable to a 45-minute run, yielding all the benefits (without the jarring) so long as your heart rate is the same. Your muscles and joints can tell the difference between the sports, but your heart can't.

At 6 feet, 175 pounds, I'm not fat, but I wouldn't mind losing a little around the middle. I'm happy to report that cycling can burn calories at the same rate as running *if* you ride fast enough. For example, during a steady ride at 16 to 17 mph, about 7½ calories are consumed each hour for every kilogram of body weight (1 kilogram equals 2.2 pounds). For me, that's about 600 calories per hour. Running at a moderate pace (7½-minute miles) burns calories at approximately the same rate. If you're a cruiser, riding at 8 to 10 mph burns 2½ calories per kilogram of body weight per hour, which is about the same as brisk walking.

But this ride is no walk. I struggle to stay with the pack, and the advice I hear makes the effort worthwhile: Ride with your hands on the brake lever hoods for comfort and control; stay about a wheel-length behind another rider to decrease wind resistance by 20 percent; shift to a lower gear *before* starting uphill; when you need to ride with one hand, hold the handlebar next to the stem to improve stability; vary your head position to avoid getting a sore neck; sit up occasionally to relieve lower-back tension; and on a warm day like this, keep drinking water.

The tips help, but suddenly it seems as if a huge magnet is pulling the other riders away. I pedal harder but can't catch up. One of the editors drops back to see if I'm okay. A bit embarrassed, I tell him I'm fine and that he should go on without me. In a moment I'm alone.

I grope my way along the back roads, coasting when I can. I ride through little towns I've only driven past before—places

I've seen but never *seen*. An old couple eats apples on a porch. A woman folds laundry under a weeping willow. An old man turns off his lawn mower to give me directions. The world spins at the speed of my bicycle wheel.

When I finally roll into the office parking lot, I'm exhausted but excited. I used to think bicycling was more a cult than a sport. I was awed by its strange language and clothes. But back in the bike shop, I realize the lingo and Lycra are secondary. What matters is having a good ride. This one was tough, but that's certainly nothing to be afraid of. I'll get better. Cycling will get easier.

This book is designed with that goal in mind. It'll acquaint you with the mechanics of bicycling and all the necessary equipment. It'll teach you basic riding techniques and how to get the most enjoyment from your miles. Plus, you'll learn how to set goals and train for various events. In all, it's a comprehensive primer for beginning cyclists.

Tomorrow I'm going to buy myself a pair of those black shorts. I'm also going to get a pair of cycling shoes—45s, of course. And then I'm going out for another ride, because, as you'll soon discover, there's something wonderfully addictive about this sport.

Nelson Pena, Editor
Bicycling Magazine

Part One
FIRST BIKE

1 CHOOSING THE RIGHT BIKE

Maybe the glamour and heroics of the Tour de France are what got you thinking about buying a bike. Or will bicycling for you be a practical, cheap alternative to gridlock and parking decks? Perhaps it's the adventure of pedaling a go-anywhere mountain bike along secluded forest trails or the allure of seeing the country from the seat of a touring bike that's got you thumbing these pages. Or will a bicycle be your salvation from shin splints or long lines at the health club? Maybe you're hoping to buy into a lifestyle you'll stick with long enough to finally get in shape.

Whatever the reason, you couldn't have picked a better time to join this lifetime sport that has 45 million adult participants in the United States. There's more value and performance packed into today's bikes than ever before. Plus, there are more styles of bikes for everything from racing and touring to urban commuting and backcountry exploring.

Though a bicycle's relative value has never been higher, neither has the price you'll pay for one. A quality, functional, no-frills bike costs at least $300. The quality of the bike increases proportionally with price to around $600 or $700, at which point the extra money starts buying increasingly subtle refinements in the frame and components that are important only to advanced cyclists.

Forget the $79 department-store special. It's suitable for a few years of abuse by a growing child, but its weight and inferior quality will soon dampen your enthusiasm. Instead,

1

look in bike shops, where there are quality products and skilled personnel who will help you select a bike that fits your body and needs.

A good entry-level bike should have a strong but light frame made of steel alloy or aluminum; wheels with aluminum alloy rims (they're actually stronger than steel and make the bike accelerate, handle, and stop better); sealed or shielded bearings to keep the hubs and pedals turning smoothly without frequent maintenance; powerful brakes that don't grab; and a foolproof gear-changing system with shift levers that have audible click stops. Such "index shifting" systems were introduced a few years ago and are now used by all levels of cyclists. They make shifting as easy as tuning a push-button car radio.

Surveying the Market

Mountain bikes. If you're still referring to models with upright handlebars as "3-speeds" and those with derailleurs as "10-speeds," you've got some catching up to do. The flat (as opposed to downturned or "drop") handlebar and heads-up riding position of the old 3-speed is still around, but now it's usually complemented with fat (1.5 inches or wider), low-pressure, knobby tires and a 15-, 18-, or even 21-speed gear system with bar-mounted shifters.

Such mountain or all-terrain bikes (ATBs) are the most popular style these days. Though designed for riding on challenging, unpaved terrain, most mountain bikes seldom see such severe use. Instead, they're bought for their comfortable ride (the wide tires absorb road shock), durability, and wide-range gearing, which makes hill climbing comparatively easy, on or off pavement. Most mountain bikes are designed to accept load-carrying racks, which makes them popular with urban commuters. Lots of tire styles for their 26-inch-diameter wheels are available, from wide, heavily lugged tread patterns, for maximum traction in dirt, to narrow, smooth-treaded, high-pressure models, for efficient street cruising.

However, riders who pedal nonstop for several hours often discover that comfort is inversely proportional to saddle time, and the mountain bike's heavier weight and higher rolling resistance make it significantly less efficient on pavement than a traditional road bike.

Consequently, a fast 20-mile ride on a nimble road bike can be less demanding physically than grinding out the same distance more slowly on a mountain bike. Indeed, when mountain bikers join organized 100-mile road rides, it's common to find them still struggling through the last miles after the roadies have crossed the line, swapped adventures, gone home, showered, and cracked the tabs of a few cold frothy ones. Smooth-treaded mountain bike tires lessen the performance gap, but many shops are seeing customers who previously bought ATBs for all-purpose use coming back to add a road bike.

Since this category includes a range of bikes—from laid-back, bombproof city models to ultralight, quick-handling, costly racers—you should match the style to your type of riding. Generally, you can find a reasonable degree of all-around performance near the bottom of the price scale. As the bikes get more expensive, you gain better frame tubing and craftsmanship, more durable and smoother-working components, a lighter overall weight, and a more elaborate paint job.

If urban riding with a bit of weekend trail exploration is your style, then look for a model with a wheelbase of 42 inches or more, chainstays that measure 17 inches or longer, and a fork rake of 2 inches. If gonzo trail riding or off-road racing is your calling, then you'll need a bike with more aggressive handling characteristics. Look for one with a wheelbase of 41 inches, seat tube angles of 71 to 74 degrees, head tube angles of 69 to 72 degrees, and a fork rake less than 2 inches.

Road bikes. Road bikes with derailleurs and skinny tires— what used to be called 10-speeds—are still popular for racing, touring, and fitness cycling, but you'll be hard-pressed to find one with only ten gears. The norm is 12 speeds for recreational riding and 14 or 16 for racing.

Don't be misled by the term "racing bike." You don't need a competitive bone in your body to appreciate spirited performance. In fact, most racing-bike riders, like most sports car owners, don't race. Except for a few special-purpose machines with ultraquick steering, a racing bike requires no more skill to ride than a recreational model and is not significantly less

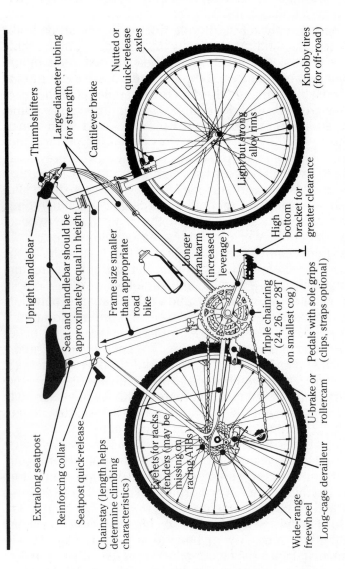

Illustration 1-1. The anatomy of a mountain bike.

Thumbshifters

Large-diameter tubing for strength

Nutted or quick-release axles

Cantilever brake

Knobby tires (for off-road)

Light but strong alloy rims

Upright handlebar

Seat and handlebar should be approximately equal in height

Frame size smaller than appropriate road bike

Longer crankarm (increased leverage)

High bottom bracket for greater clearance

Triple chainring (24, 26, or 28T on smallest cog)

Pedals with sole grips (clips, straps optional)

Extralong seatpost

Reinforcing collar

Seatpost quick-release

Chainstay (length helps determine climbing characteristics)

Eyelets for racks, fenders (may be missing on racing ATBs)

U-brake or rollercam

Wide-range freewheel

Long-cage derailleur

comfortable, but its greater efficiency allows you to cover more distance more quickly. It's a good choice for any reasonably fit cyclist who wants to get the most distance and speed out of his or her pedaling effort, and who doesn't require the carrying capacity or superlow gears of a touring bike. It's an obvious choice for anyone contemplating entering races or triathlons.

You can get a racing bike with a high degree of performance without spending a lot of money. As with mountain bikes, you generally get higher-quality components, lighter frame materials, more attentive construction, and better paint jobs as you move up the price scale.

What makes a bike a racer? Frame geometry is the primary factor. Although a bike can't be judged solely by its dimensions, certain measurements can convey its purpose. The quickest-handling racing bikes have short (38- or 39-inch) wheelbases, steep (74-degree or greater) head and seat tube angles, high (10.5-inch-plus) bottom brackets, and short (less than 1.5-inch) fork rakes.

Slacker head and seat tube angles and longer wheelbases generally result in a bike that's more stable, smoother riding, and better suited for longer rides and road races rather than short, tight criteriums.

Many bikes in this category have a 42-tooth small chainring, a 52T large ring, and a 13–23 or 13–24T freewheel cluster. This provides a selection of gears suitable for a fit rider in hilly terrain. If you're just starting to get into shape or ride in a mountainous region, lower gears are more appropriate and can often be substituted by the dealer.

Another type of road bike is the sport/touring model. It encompasses a range of bikes from "almost racing" to "land cruisers." Sport/touring bikes generally use frame tubing and components that are heavier and less expensive, so the prices for such models are usually the lowest of any category. However, you can spend more than $1,000 for a top-quality loaded touring bike.

Touring bikes usually have gearing similar to that of mountain bikes (three chainrings, five to seven cogs), thus enabling riders to climb big hills with heavy loads. Such bikes are also a good choice for riders who don't need the carrying capacity but do require low gears for hilly terrain. Their drawback, however, is a slower ride and less agile handling compared to the more nimble sport and racing bikes. This is because their frames are designed for maximum stability with heavy loads.

Generally, touring bikes have the longest wheelbases (40 inches or more), chainstays, and fork rakes of any model. They are designed to remain stable when carrying front and rear loads. They may have such amenities as cantilever brakes for added stopping power, extra braze-ons for a third water bottle cage, and low-riding front racks.

If you're interested in fast recreational riding and an occasional century, the racy end of the sport/touring group may be more your style. High-performance sport bikes have lower gearing than all-out racers, plus slightly longer wheelbases and chainstays to make them more stable. Many have braze-ons for racks, so you can carry some gear if you wish. Most sport bikes can also accommodate fenders for foul-weather riding.

Hybrid and women's bikes. Hybrid bikes are a relatively new innovation. They're half road/half mountain bike in that they roll well on pavement yet can handle all but the roughest backwoods terrain. Generally, hybrids feature stout frames, wider (up to 1.5-inch) tires on 26- or 27-inch wheels, cantilever brakes, triple cranksets, and either drop or straight mountain-bike–style handlebars. As with ATBs, the shift levers are located on the handlebar, either as bar-ends or thumbshifters. As such, they're good choices for cyclists who ride both on and off pavement yet can afford only one bike. Such versatility has made them one of the fastest growing styles of bike.

So-called women's bikes are designed to meet the needs of smaller riders. For instance, women generally have shorter torsos and arms, relative to their height, than men. They also have a wider pelvis and tend not to be as tall. These differences mean that conventional bikes may not fit some women as well as they should.

The most common problem is top tube length. If a woman's leg length is such that she needs a 23-inch frame, for example, she may find that its 22-inch top tube and long stem put her too far forward. And substituting a shorter stem won't completely cure the awkward feeling. Thus, smaller women

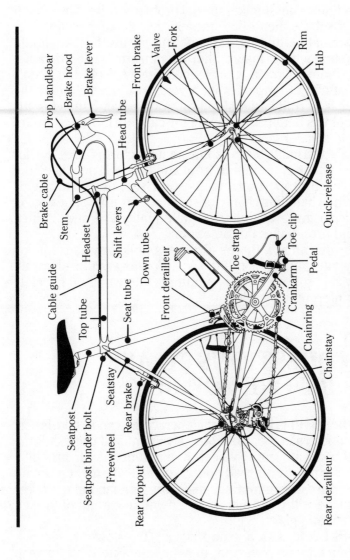

Illustration1-2. The anatomy of a road bike.

should pay special attention to top tube length when shopping for a bike. Likewise, a woman's wider pelvis should be supported by a wider saddle.

As frames get smaller, special problems arise. The person riding a sub-20-inch bike probably has smaller hands, narrower shoulders, and shorter legs. This means the bike should have components to match. Shorter crankarms (165mm rather than 170mm) allow a short-legged rider to spin the pedals more naturally. Compact brake levers, positioned closer to the handlebar, permit easier stopping. A narrower handlebar fits the shoulders better. And smaller toe clips are more accommodating to smaller feet.

On extrasmall bikes, some manufacturers use smaller wheels—either in front or in front and back—to help keep the bike's frame proportional to its short seat tube. This helps maintain its handling characteristics and "normal" appearance. The increasing availability of high-quality 26- and 24-inch rims and tires makes this an option.

As you can see, there's a variety of bikes available today for any age, ability, or riding style. Whatever your pleasure, from racing to touring to commuting, you can do it in safety and comfort on a bicycle.

▪2 QUESTIONS TO ASK BEFORE YOU BUY

Where will I ride? An efficient racing or sport bike is best for the open road. For riding on pavement and packed dirt, a touring bike with sturdy wheels or a mountain or hybrid bike will do. For mostly off-road riding, you'll need a true mountain bike. For urban commuting, ATBs are popular, but a road or hybrid bike will work just as well if you're careful of broken pavement and glass.

Will I ride with a group? If not, the slower speed of a mountain bike on pavement may be fine. But trying to keep pace with road bikes when you're pumping the pedals of a fat-tire ATB could discourage you from group riding altogether.

Do I need carrying capacity? High-performance road

and mountain bikes often lack eyelets for attaching racks, as well as the stable handling required to carry heavy loads. If you haul more gear than will fit in a handlebar or seat bag, buy a bike with dropout eyelets.

How fit am I? If you're already fit for cycling, you can handle the high, closely spaced gears of a racing bike. If you're not that fit but your goal is to become so, a racing or sport bike is still appropriate if you choose one with a moderate gear range or substitute a wider-range freewheel. If you have no interest in riding hard and fast and want to pedal as painlessly as possible, the wide range and ultralow bottom gear of a touring or mountain bike is for you. If you plan on touring with a heavy load, you'll need similar low gears even if you're racer-fit.

How hilly is the terrain in my area? The steeper and/or longer the hills, the more you'll appreciate a freewheel with large, low-gear cogs. Avoid any bike that has a freewheel the diameter of a corn cob.

How devoted a cyclist will I be? You'll be disappointed at the performance of a low-budget bike intended for short recreational rides if you try to push it farther or faster. Conversely, an expensive road or mountain bike designed for the rigors of competition is a waste for casual weekend tootling on local bike paths. Nevertheless, if you expect cycling to become an increasingly important part of your life, it pays to buy a better bike than your current fitness requires. Thus, as you progress as a rider, you'll still own a suitable steed.

3 SIZING A NEW BIKE

A bicycle's saddle and handlebar are adjustable, but its frame has fixed dimensions. If the tube lengths aren't carefully matched to your body proportions, you won't achieve a comfortable and efficient riding position. Thus, it is essential to determine which frame size is best after deciding which bike model to buy.

For the answer we turned to Paul Brown, who runs the Cycle Dynamics bike shop in Novato, California. The sizing procedure presented here is a simplification of the method he uses to measure customers for custom frames. It requires just three measurements. (See illustration 1-3.) Ask a friend to help you.

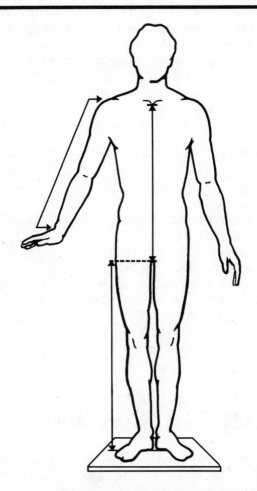

Illustration 1-3. Carefully make these three measurements, then use the tables on page 12 to determine your ideal bike size.

Inseam length. Stand with your bare feet 6 inches apart. With a tape measure, measure the distance from your crotch to the floor. This is your inseam length.

Torso length. Find the top of your sternum, which is the notch between your collarbones, just below the Adam's apple. The distance from your crotch to the top of the sternum is your torso length.

Arm length. Straighten your arm and hold it to the side. Measure from the point of your shoulder (acromion) to the point where your wrist pivots when you bend your hand backward.

Table 1-1 shows the frame size, bottom bracket height, and crankarm length that match your inseam length. Table 1-2 shows the proper top tube length and stem extension for your torso-plus-arm length. These are the key dimensions for a road-racing bicycle. A loaded touring bike should have a frame approximately 1 inch larger with a top tube 1 inch shorter than listed for the respective body measurements. A sport bike should be somewhere in between, depending on whether you emphasize fast recreational riding or light touring. The tables don't work for mountain bikes, which are an entirely different design. (In general, there should be several inches of clearance between your crotch and the top tube when straddling a mountain bike. The correct size will be about 3 inches smaller than that of your ideal road bike.)

Although the numbers are calculated to the nearest tenth of an inch, this is not a precise science. Anything within an inch should fit well. The human body is adaptable, and a bike saddle is adjustable. A handlebar stem can be replaced with one that fits better.

As you measure various bikes of the same frame size, you'll probably find different top tube lengths. If you have long legs and a short upper body, look for a bike with a shorter-than-average top tube. If you have a disproportionately long torso, find a bike with a longer-than-average top tube.

TABLE 1-1.
Getting the Right Fit—1

Inseam Length (in.)	Recom- mended Frame Size (in.)	Recom- mended Bottom Bracket Height (in.)	Recom- mended Crank Length (mm.)
28	18.5	10.1	160–165
29	19.5	10.1	160–165
30	20.4	10.3	165–167.5
31	21.2	10.3	165–167.5
32	22.0	10.5	170
33	22.6	10.5	170
34	23.3	10.6	170–172.5
35	24.0	10.6	170–172.5
36	24.7	10.7	172.5–175
37	25.4	10.7	172.5–175
38	26.1	10.8	175–177.5
39	26.8	10.8	175–177.5
40	27.5	11.0	177.5–180
41	28.2	11.0	177.5–180
42	28.9	11.1	180

NOTES:

1.   Frame size is measured along the seat tube from the center of the crank axle to the top of the top tube.

2.   With Shimano Dyna-Drive cranks and pedals or AeroLite pedals, subtract ½ inch from the frame size.

3.   With Look pedals, add ½ inch to the frame size.

4.   If using a crank length other than that shown for your inseam, add or subtract the appropriate difference for frame size. 2.5 mm = 0.1 inch.

5.   It is not practical to make a conventional bicycle for an inseam less than 28 inches. Look for a model with a small front wheel or a sloping top tube if this is the case.

TABLE 1-2.
Getting the Right Fit—2

Torso + Arm Length (in.)	Recommended Top Tube Length (in.)	Recommended Stem Extension (mm.)
40	19.5	90
41	19.9	90
42	20.3	90
43	20.6	90
44	21.0	90
45	21.3	90
46	21.6	100
47	21.9	100
48	22.2	100
49	22.5	100
50	22.8	100
51	23.1	100
52	23.4	100
53	23.7	100

NOTES:
1. Top tube length is measured from the centerline of the head tube to the centerline of the seat tube.

2. Stem length is measured from the center of the expander bolt to the center of the handlebar.

3. It's the combination of top tube length and stem extension that matters, so the correct reach is attainable by using a stem that's one centimeter longer with a top tube that's one centimeter shorter, for example.

■4 CLOTHING AND ACCESSORY CHECKLIST

Once you buy a bicycle, you still aren't quite ready to ride. Some accessories are essential, while others just make cycling more enjoyable. Use the following checklist, arranged in order of priority, to ensure that you're properly equipped.

Helmet. *Bicycling* magazine receives numerous letters from cyclists who walked away from spills that might have resulted in serious head injuries if they had not been wearing a helmet.

It's easier than ever to protect yourself, because many modern helmets are light, well ventilated, and attractive. Wearing one might feel strange at first, but it will soon become as natural as fastening a car's seat belt. Look for an ANSI and/or Snell Foundation sticker inside the helmet, which indicates that it meets accepted impact standards. It should fit snugly without being tight. Try on several brands, because there are many different shapes. Choosing a helmet that looks good means you'll enjoy wearing it. A bonus is that motorists usually view helmeted riders as law-abiding and responsible.

Emergency items. A seat bag, which attaches under the saddle, is an inconspicuous and handy way to store emergency items. Yours should include one or two spare inner tubes, a patch kit, a couple of tire levers, identification, and some change for a phone call should all else fail. Also, you'll need a frame-fit pump or a quick-fill pressurized cartridge to inflate the spare. A pump that affixes under the top tube leaves the down and seat tubes free for mounting water bottles. See chapter 15 for tips on changing a flat tire. It's easy.

Water bottle and cage. These will sometimes be included in the purchase price of your bicycle. If not, buy two of each. Fluid intake is essential when riding, especially on hot days.

Shorts. Cycling shorts are available in touring and racing models. Both have a seamless piece of material, called a chamois (natural or synthetic), sewn into the seat. It provides a smooth, padded surface where you contact the saddle and reduces chafing. Cyclists generally don't wear anything underneath such shorts, although seamless undershorts are available.

Another advantage of cycling shorts is that they're built to move with you, as opposed to regular shorts that can pinch and bind. Touring shorts may have pockets on the sides of the legs, rather than the front, to prevent irritation from items such as keys. Some pockets are zippered or snapped to keep items from falling out.

Racing-style shorts are made of body-hugging fabrics such as nylon or Lycra. These are generally pocketless, although some have a key holder sewn into the waist. They should fit snugly without being tight. The more contoured fabric panels, the better the fit. (Eight panels signifies premium quality.)

Your shorts should be cleaned frequently, especially during warm weather, to prevent rashes and sores. Buy a second pair so you'll have one to wear when the other is being washed.

Shoes. Cycling shoes have a stiff sole that distributes the pressure of the sharp pedal edges over the length of the foot. This helps you ride longer and stronger, while preventing foot fatigue and soreness. Most beginners start with touring shoes, which are cousins of running shoes. They're stiff enough for efficient pedaling but flexible enough for walking short distances. Besides an internal plastic or metal sole stiffener, touring shoes have reinforced uppers that resist stretching and prevent irritation from toe clips and straps.

Performance-oriented beginners may prefer cleated shoes. These connect your feet solidly to the pedals, thereby enhancing pedaling efficiency. Despite the locked-in feel, they're safe and easy to use. Be sure, however, to have the cleat position set correctly by the dealer, or you may injure your knees.

Gloves. Cycling gloves are an important piece of safety equipment because in a fall, your hands naturally go out to protect your body. Their thick, padded palms will prevent cuts and bruises. Gloves also distribute the pressure of the handlebar across your palms, thereby preventing blisters, chafing, and nerve compression. You can choose from models with gel or water bladder cushioning. Look for tight, even seams that won't unravel. A good fit, without binding or tightness, is important. Try different brands, since some will fit better than others.

Tools. A few tools will enable you to handle most minor repairs and adjustments. Allen wrenches (4, 5, and 6mm), a flat-head and Phillips screwdriver, and a spoke wrench (sized to your spoke nipples) will suffice. Several manufacturers combine these tools and others into a convenient, compact kit that fits in a saddle bag. You'll need a can of chain lube, too.

Photograph 1-1. There is a wide variety of cycling clothing and accessories to make your ride safer and more comfortable.

Eyewear. Sports eyewear becomes more popular each year, and for good reason. Sunglasses offer protection from wind, bugs, grit, glare, and ultraviolet light. Look for sports eyewear that wraps around the field of vision, permitting a good peripheral view. The lenses should be distortion-free and made of a high-impact, shatterproof material. A neutral gray or green tint is best for bright daylight, while clear or amber lenses are recommended for bad weather.

Jersey. Cycling jerseys have several advantages over T-shirts. They're made of fabrics that wick moisture away from the body to speed evaporation. During cool weather this prevents you from feeling cold and clammy, while during warm weather it keeps you from overheating. The stretchy fabrics are cut in panels to match the contour of the body in a cycling position. This enhances comfort. Jerseys also have pockets in the back where you can stash extra clothing or snacks. Pick a light, bright color for maximum visibility.

Cool-weather gear. The cooler the weather in your area, the more money you'll have to spend for the proper clothing. Good first items to buy are cycling tights, a long-sleeved jersey made of a wicking, insulating fabric, and a windbreaker. These items will extend your riding into the 50-degree temperature range. To stay comfortable in colder conditions, you'll need underwear made of a wicking, insulating fabric, a few layers of insulating clothing, and a windproof jacket. Also important are winter cycling gloves and windproof shoe covers.

Part Two
FIRST MILES

5 THE PRINCIPLES OF PEDALING

Cycling has come a long way in the past few years. Today's bicycles are better and faster. They're also no longer just for kids. In fact, according to the Bicycle Institute of America, there are now more adults than children riding bikes.

With so many people rediscovering the bicycle, it's probably a good time to review some basic guidelines. Chances are, you'll remember your mother or father yelling some of these same instructions as you wobbled down the driveway. Only then you were too excited to listen closely and in too much of a youthful hurry to ask why.

Ride with traffic. Although it might seem safer to pedal against traffic so you can see approaching vehicles, nothing is more dangerous. First, it's confusing to motorists, especially at intersections where, for example, they aren't conditioned to look for vehicles approaching from the right when making a right-hand turn. Second, if a car is going 40 mph and you're pedaling toward it at 20 mph, you're approaching each other at 60 mph. If, however, you're traveling in the same direction, the car approaches at only 20 mph and the driver has more time to see and respond to you. Last, and most important, cyclists are legally required to follow the same traffic rules as motor vehicles in all states.

Behave predictably. Don't zip in and out of traffic, run red lights, hop curbs, or try to outsprint drivers. Think of the things that irritate you most about cyclists when you're driving, and don't do them. When you're making a turn, get in the proper lane, signal your intention, and if the intersection is a busy one, wait your turn. If you respect the rules of the road and the rights of motorists, they will respect you.

Ride defensively. Stay alert and anticipate the actions of motorists. Lift your nose off the handlebar and analyze traffic situations, just as you do while driving. One trick is to look drivers directly in the eye at intersections. This will tell you if they're daydreaming or if they know you're there.

Use your ears as well as your eyes. Listen for approaching vehicles. With practice, you'll be able to hear trucks and cars approaching from far away, and even gauge how close they might come to you. Never wear Walkman-type headphones because they deprive you of this valuable sense. In fact, they're illegal for cycling in some states.

Should a motorist cut you off or yell something at you, resist the urge to make an obscene gesture or shout profanities. Remember, you're dealing with a machine that can kill or maim you, and a driver who may even be carrying a weapon.

Wear a helmet. We know, we know . . . you never wore a helmet as a kid and you took your share of spills without cracking your skull. Plus, the thing will probably make you self-conscious.

Consider, however, that at least 1,000 people die every year from cycling accidents, and 85 percent of these fatalities stem from head trauma. Helmets can reduce the risk of head injury by nearly 80 percent. Consider also that you're riding in a much different fashion than when you were a kid. Your head is higher from the ground and will impact with greater force. Your speed is faster, too. Helmets are no longer the inverted soup bowls they were a few years ago, either. They're light, airy, color-coordinated, and are even required in many cycling events, including all amateur races. Take one for a test ride and see if you don't forget it's there after a few minutes.

Learn to keep your bike in good working order. You'll enjoy the sport more if you understand and have confidence in the mechanical workings of your bicycle. Learn how to change a flat tire and make minor adjustments and repairs. For tips, consult your bike shop or a friend, or purchase a good repair manual. We publish *Bicycling Magazine's Complete Guide to Bicycle Maintenance and Repair,* and the smaller paperback, *Bicycling Magazine's Basic Maintenance and Repair.*

Vary your riding. Nothing is more boring than riding the same route day after day at the same speed and time. Map different routes, ride them at different times of day, and occasionally cycle with people who are a little stronger, faster, and more experienced. In this way, you'll stay mentally fresh, learn a lot, and become stronger and faster.

Likewise, supplement your cycling with other activities. Good complementary sports are running, swimming, cross-country skiing, and rowing. These sports work muscles that cycling neglects and will heighten your overall fitness level. For instance, cycling emphasizes the muscles in the front of your legs (quadriceps). To balance their development and insulate yourself against injury, try running to condition the muscles in the back of the legs (hamstrings).

Consume enough calories. The more physically active you are, the more fuel your body needs. Therefore, don't cut calories in the belief that cycling *and* dieting will help you get in shape and lose weight quicker. If you do, you're liable to become fatigued or even sick. For instance, a 175-pound person riding at 16 mph typically uses 600 calories an hour. In the course of a 50-mile ride, this same person will burn about 2,000 calories, which represents the amount in three average meals. While this doesn't give you a license to replenish on Big Macs and bonbons, it does permit you to eat well without feeling guilty and still lose excess weight. For the most energy, eat natural foods that are rich in carbohydrate and low in fat.

Keep a training diary. To gauge improvement and provide added training incentive, keep a record of your cycling. After every ride, record mileage, elapsed time, average speed, type of terrain, weather, even the gears used. Most important, assess how you felt while riding and rate yourself on a one-to-five scale. You can expand your diary by keeping track of such other variables as hours slept, foods eaten, weight, and waking pulse rate. By periodically assessing the information in your training diary, you'll get to know your body better and be able to draw direct correlations to performance.

Be patient. Naturally, you're excited about your new sport and anxious to improve. But don't try to do too much too soon or you'll sap your enthusiasm and maybe even injure yourself. Start slowly and set attainable short-range goals. If your knees begin aching, back off. Keep things in perspective and realize that you're not training for the Tour de France. In time, continue to challenge yourself by resetting these goals. But remember that the harder and farther you ride, the more rest you need. View a day or even a week away from the bike as a part of your training, not an interruption to it.

6 LEARNING THE LINGO

Cycling has an entire language of its own. When a friend says she's planning a roller workout, don't expect to see curlers. When you're offered a pull, don't ask where to attach the towline. When you're called a wheelsucker, don't . . . well, you get the idea. To help avoid embarrassing situations, here's a page from the bikie's dictionary.

Attack. To accelerate suddenly, pulling away from other riders.

Block. To legally impede the progress of riders in the pack to allow teammates in the break a better chance to stay away.

Bonk. To completely run out of energy, or as marathoners say, "hit the wall." Occurs when glycogen stores are exhausted.

Break or breakaway. One or more cyclists who leave the main group of riders behind by going "off the front."

Cadence. The rate of pedaling measured in revolutions per minute (rpm) for one of your feet.

Cat I, II, III, IV. Racing categories designated by the U.S. Cycling Federation, based on a rider's ability and/or experience, with I's having the most and IV's the least.

Century. A 100-mile ride.

Circuit race. A multilap road race on a course 2 miles or more in length.

Clincher. A tire with a detachable inner tube.

Criterium. A multilap event on a course that's usually 1 mile or less in length.

Domestique. A rider who sacrifices individual performance to work for the team leaders.

Draft. To ride closely behind another rider in order to reduce wind resistance.

Checkout Receipt
Mount Laurel Library

Title: Bicycling Magazine's New
Bike Owner'
Call Number: 796.6 Bic
Item ID: 36242000574828
Date Due: 2/14/2020

Renew your items online:
http://www.mountlaurellibrary.org

Dropped. A term used to describe a rider who failed to keep pace with the group he was riding in.

Drops. The part of the handlebar below the brake levers. Also called hooks.

Echelon. A type of paceline in which riders angle themselves across the road in order to get the maximum draft in a crosswind.

Field sprint. A sprint to the finish by the main group of riders.

Fred. Derisive term used by cycling snobs to describe novice riders or tourists.

Full tuck. An extremely crouched riding position used for fast descents.

General classification. A rider's overall standing in a stage race. Also called g.c.

Gorp. A high-carbohydrate snack made from nuts, seeds, raisins, granola, candy, and so on. An acronym for "good ol' raisins and peanuts."

Granny. The lowest or easiest gear on a bicycle.

Hammer. To ride as hard as possible. Also known as jamming.

Hang in. To barely maintain contact at the back of the pack.

Honk. To stand on the pedals with your hands on the brake lever hoods while climbing.

Hook. To deliberately move your back wheel into the front wheel of a pursuing rider.

Jump. A quick, hard acceleration.

Leadout. A race tactic in which a rider accelerates to maximum speed so a teammate can draft and then sprint past to the finish.

Metric century. A 100-kilometer (62-mile) ride.

Minuteman. In a time trial, the rider who immediately precedes you in the starting order. So called because in most time trials, riders start at 1-minute intervals.

Motor pace. To ride in the draft of a motorcycle or car in order to train in a big gear at 25 to 35 mph.

Off the back. A term used to describe one or more riders who have failed to keep pace with the main group.

Off the front. A term used to describe one or more riders who have left the main group behind.

Overgear. To use a gear too big for the terrain or your level of fitness.

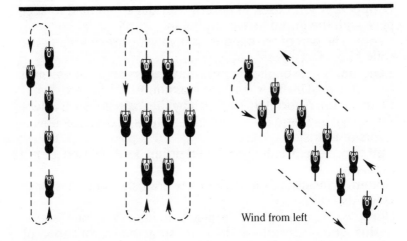

Illustration 2-1. From left to right, a single paceline formation, a double paceline, and an echelon.

Paceline. A single-file group formation in which each rider takes a turn breaking the wind at the front before pulling aside, dropping to the rear position, and recovering in the draft until reaching the front again.

Peloton. A large cluster of riders. Also called a pack, field, or bunch.

Pizza elbow. *See* Road rash.

Prime. A prize or time bonus awarded to the winner of selected laps during a criterium or track race. It may also be given to the first rider reaching a certain point in a road race. Pronounced "preem."

Pull. To take a turn leading a group of riders. Also referred to as pulling through.

Pusher. A rider who pedals a big gear with a relatively slow cadence.

Road rash. Any skin abrasion resulting from a fall.

Rollers. An indoor training device for bicycles that works somewhat like a treadmill.

Saddle time. Time spent cycling.

Sag wagon. A motor vehicle that follows a group of riders, carrying equipment and lending assistance in the event of difficulty. Sometimes called a broom wagon.

Sew-up. A tire with an encased inner tube. Also called a tubular.

Sit on a wheel. To ride directly behind someone in order to benefit from his slipstream. Also known as sitting in or wheelsucking.

Slingshot. To sprint around a rider after taking advantage of his slipstream.

Snap. The ability to accelerate quickly.

Soft-pedal. To rotate the pedals without actually applying power.

Spin. To pedal at high cadence.

Spinner. A rider who pedals in a moderate gear at a relatively fast cadence.

Squirrel. A nervous or unstable rider.

Stage race. A multiday event, such as the Tour de France, that consists of point-to-point and circuit road races, time trials, and sometimes criteriums. The winner is the rider with the lowest elapsed time for all stages.

Stayer. A rider with the ability to pedal at a relatively high speed for long periods. Also called a pacer.

Take a flyer. To suddenly sprint away from the group.

Tempo. Fast riding at a brisk cadence.

Throwing the bike. A racing technique in which a rider pushes the bike ahead of his body at the finish, hoping to edge another sprinting rider.

Time trial. A race against the clock over a set distance.

Tops. The section of handlebar between the stem and brake levers.

Track bike. A bike with no braking or shifting mechanisms. Used for riding on a velodrome.

Turkey. An unskilled cyclist.

Velodrome. An oval track with banked corners. Used for a variety of races.

Wheelsucker. Someone who rides behind others and doesn't take a pull.

Wind-up. Steady acceleration to an all-out effort.

7 YOUR FIRST RIDING LESSON

Enough chitchat. It's time to stop reading about cycling and start doing it. So get your bike and let's go for a quick introductory spin. Stay on our wheel and we'll show you how to shift gears, ride a straight line, corner, climb, and descend. Soon you'll be riding like a pro.

But wait! We're not ready yet. You wouldn't drive a car on a cold winter morning without warming it up, would you? For your body, every day is a cold winter morning. You've got to warm it up to prevent stalling.

Before every ride, stretch for 5 to 10 minutes. To loosen your back muscles, gently turn your torso back and forth while standing with your arms extended and legs apart. To stretch the muscles in the front of your legs (quadriceps), stand on one leg, bend the other knee back, and grasp your foot. Slowly pull it toward your rear end, then repeat for the other leg. To loosen the muscles in the back of your legs (hamstrings), sit on the floor with one leg extended and the other tucked in so the sole of your foot faces the inside of your thigh. Then try to touch the toes of your extended leg. Repeat for the other leg.

These are just a few examples of stretching exercises. Whatever ones you do, always stretch with smooth, gentle movements. Hold each stretch for 20 to 30 seconds so the muscles have the opportunity to relax in the extended position. If it starts to hurt, stop.

Okay, it's time to start riding—but not too fast! Spend the first 10 to 20 minutes on the bike pedaling easily in low-resistance gears to further loosen your leg muscles. (Do the same at the end of the ride to cool down. Postride stretching helps, too.)

Shift a few times to familiarize yourself with the bike's gear system. The left shift lever controls the front derailleur and moves the chain between chainrings. Try it. Feel how much less resistance there is when the chain is on the smallest ring. This is commonly used for climbing or riding into a head wind.

Conversely, the right shift lever controls the rear derailleur and moves the chain between freewheel cogs. Feel how the resistance decreases as it moves from the smallest to the largest cog and increases as it moves in the opposite direction.

By shifting to the appropriate gear (larger cogs for climbing, smaller cogs for descending and flatland riding) you'll be able to maintain a comfortable pedaling rate or cadence and conserve energy. Got it? Good. Now we can really start moving.

Get behind us and concentrate on riding a straight line. Weaving is dangerous. It annoys fellow riders and could turn you into a motorist's hood ornament. Cycling coach Roger Young suggests focusing your eyes 20 feet ahead when riding at 10 to 15 mph, and 1 foot farther for every additional mph. Keep your wrists and elbows relaxed. Steer with your entire body, not just your arms. We'll stay on these country roads until you get the hang of it.

You're doing great. Now try working on your pedaling style. Resist the temptation to stomp on the pedals. Instead, feel and visualize your feet spinning in smooth circles. Position the balls of your feet directly over the pedal axles and choose gears that let you maintain a cadence of 90 revolutions per minute (rpm). You can calculate this by counting the number of times your right leg reaches the top of the pedal stroke in 30 seconds, then multiply by two.

At the top of each pedal revolution, push your lower leg forward from the knee. Gradually add power from the thigh, as your foot begins descending through the power stroke. Just before your foot finishes its downward journey, your lower leg should again start flexing at the knee to pull back on the pedal. This is a motion that takes practice to perfect. You don't have to pull up very hard. By reducing the weight of each leg during the upward part of the stroke, you'll help the opposite leg apply more power.

Feels good, doesn't it? Kind of makes you want to ride straight off into the sunset. Well, no road goes on forever, so eventually you'll want to turn around, and this involves learning to corner.

Up ahead we'll make a 90-degree, right-hand turn. Follow us as we check for traffic and move toward the center of the lane. Choose a line through the corner, stop pedaling with the inside pedal up, then lean your bike into the turn and coast through. Pretty exhilarating, huh? For added stability and increased rear wheel traction, try sitting toward the back of the saddle next time. And once you start turning, don't make any major change in your line or you might slip and crash.

Uh-oh. Here comes a hill. Man, is this going to be painful. Does the heartmobile come out this way? Don't worry, we're just kidding. It's really not that difficult.

Get into a lower gear now, before we start climbing, by shifting to a larger freewheel cog and/or to the small chainring. If you wait until later, your drivetrain is liable to misshift under the hard pedaling load.

Climbing style is a matter of preference. Some riders like to stay seated on long climbs, pedaling an easy gear fairly quickly. They'll have their hands apart on top of the handlebar to facilitate breathing, and their upper body will bob as they pull on the bar for leverage. Other riders prefer to do most of their climbing out of the saddle. They hook their thumbs over the brake lever hoods, stand up, and let the bike rock gently beneath them. In this way they can apply their body weight to each downward pedal stroke and push a bigger gear. Experiment with both styles to find the one that's most comfortable for you. You'll probably find that you need to alternate styles to stay fresh on long climbs.

A large part of climbing is psychological. To avoid becoming demoralized, focus on the road in front of you rather than the distant summit. Have confidence that you can make it to the top. View hills as a challenge that will make you stronger.

All right! We made it! Now comes the fun part, going *down-n-n-n-n!*

Shift to a higher gear and keep pedaling to increase stability. It gets pretty steep up ahead, so watch out. If your bike starts to shimmy, squeeze its top tube between your knees. Don't keep the brakes on all the time. Instead, pump them to control your speed.

Here comes a corner! Brake to a safe speed, pick a line, and take it as we did before—weight back, inside pedal up. We've got a few more turns, then we're at the bottom. This is what cycling is all about!

Well, that's about it for today. You really did well. Practice what you've learned and we'll see you out here again in a few days!

8 SHARING THE ROAD

It may sound crazy, but it's time cyclists start thinking of ways to make life easier for motorists. After all, it's in our own self-interest to make the road a safer, more pleasant place. Even though you probably fantasize about retaliating against rude or aggressive drivers, it's seldom an option at the time. A better policy is to minimize the chance for conflict in the first place. Here are eight easy ways to do so.

1. Keep right. This most basic rule of sharing the road with motor vehicles is the one that cyclists are most casual about. If there's a wide, clean shoulder, use it. Barring potholes, storm grates, parked cars, glass, and other hazards, most of the time it's easier (and safer) to ride to the right. One thing that always irritates motorists is a cyclist riding in the middle of the roadway for no apparent reason. Besides, why take unnecessary risks? You can never be sure the driver behind isn't a short-fused nut.

2. Use common sense about riding two or more abreast. All of us know how enjoyable it is to ride side by side with a companion and carry on a conversation. But road and traffic conditions may be such that vehicles back up behind you when they could otherwise get by. Thus, restrict side-by-side riding to quiet, secondary roads.

A good idea in any case is to allow a long backup to clear out. On a narrow, winding road, steer to the right and wave vehicles by when the path is clear.

3. Don't force vehicles to repass you needlessly. You're riding along a narrow, busy road and motorists are having trouble getting by you. There are a half-dozen cars waiting at the next red light, all of which have already patiently overtaken you. Do you maintain your place in line, or do you zip past everyone on the right so you'll get the jump when the light changes? If you do the latter, you might gain 50 feet and save a few seconds, but you'll also probably create six anti-bicyclists when they get caught behind you again.

Admittedly, the scenario becomes trickier if, by hanging back, you'll miss the light. There are two tactful ways around this: one is to move up in line only far enough to just make the light; the other is to ride to the light but move out slowly and slightly to the right when it turns green, letting the cars through the intersection first. One other courtesy at traffic lights: Avoid blocking drivers who want to turn right on red.

4. Ride predictably. This one's easy. Ride in a straight line when you're cruising, and use hand signals when turning or changing lanes.

If you're riding erratically, it's difficult for drivers to know when to pass. They may let several relatively safe opportunities go by before becoming exasperated and taking a dangerous chance.

Hand signals are a courtesy and an important part of safe cycling. Motorists feel more comfortable dealing with cyclists who communicate their intentions. More important, drivers tend to show them more respect.

5. Avoid busy roads. It's surprising how often you see cyclists on a busy highway, ruffling the delicate feathers of already edgy commuters. An alternate route doesn't have to be a residential street with stop signs every quarter mile or a glass-littered, jogger-strewn bike path. Examine a detailed map of your area and you'll probably be surprised at the many quiet roads available nearby.

6. Make yourself visible. In conditions where motorists might not readily see you (an overcast day, for example), it's a courtesy and plain good sense to wear brightly colored clothes. Drivers will never blame themselves when they almost pull into your path after a too-casual look. Yes, it's unfair, but you can greatly enhance your safety by dressing to be seen.

At night, it's a different story. Drivers who encounter cyclists riding without lights and reflectors are right to consider them menaces.

7. Be careful about "provocative" actions. At a red light, even friendly drivers are likely to be irritated by a cyclist riding in circles in front of them. Many view it as a challenge to their right-of-way, even when none is intended. Similarly, if you lean on a vehicle at a stoplight, be aware that most drivers consider their cars extensions of themselves. You wouldn't want someone leaning on your bike, would you?

8. Return the favor. Cyclists come to appreciate little unexpected courtesies from motorists. For instance, we all nod a thank-you to the driver who has the right-of-way but waves us through anyway. Try returning the favor. You might, for example, motion a driver to make his turn in front of you if you'll be slow getting under way. Who knows? That driver might look a bit more favorably on the next cyclist down the road.

9 HOW TO OUT-PSYCH HOSTILE DRIVERS

Picture this: You're spinning along a deserted country road, 10 miles into a beautiful midmorning ride. Suddenly, a car approaches quickly from behind, horn blaring, then passes within inches of your bike. As it speeds away, you notice the driver watching his rearview mirror. What would you do?

The immediate reaction of most aggressive cyclists would be a rapid and forceful extension of the middle finger. Another response, one favored by the less stout of heart, would be a meek retreat to the side of the road to collect your wits. Still other cyclists would continue riding as if nothing happened.

The first two responses actually do more harm than good. To understand why, take a close look at the highway hooligan. He's not having a nice day (or life) and he wants to make sure you don't either. He harasses you, then watches for your reaction. How much fun he derives from his reckless behavior is directly related to how you respond.

Cyclists who answer with profane gestures or shouts may think they're doling out punishment, but psychologists tell us otherwise. Although you may believe the driver will be hurt or offended by your waggling finger, it actually tells him he has succeeded. Thus, inadvertently, you're rewarding the road rogue's behavior and encouraging him to do more of the same.

A timid rider who pulls off the road is also fueling the ego of the hostile driver. Although it may seem a logical way to quell the unsettling rush of adrenaline, such a retreat proves that your ride has been ruined. For the driver, it's another form of reward. In fact, the smug satisfaction he derives from it may cause him to up the ante in the future: drive faster, come closer. Someone could get hurt—or killed.

There are things you might do, such as throwing a water bottle or kicking a fender, but such incidents usually happen so fast there's no time to react. Once in a while, you may even come upon your antagonist farther up the road. These are the times when some cyclists seek revenge, either by calling the police or enacting a bit of "frontier justice." For example, there's the story of one cyclist who was harassed and then knocked into a ditch by a truck passing so close it grazed his elbow. A few miles later, he came upon the same truck parked at a roadside diner. When the driver later returned to his rig, his keys had mysteriously disappeared. Trying to play a bicycling David to the motoring Goliath, however, is usually ill-advised. In most instances it'll just incite the giant into making another, more manic pass.

The best course of action, no matter how much pride you must swallow, is still to do nothing. As the hostile driver goes by, continue in a straight line and convey no outward sign of trouble. Rather than getting angry, stay cool, and memorize the vehicle's license plate number. Chant it for the next 10 miles if necessary, or use a mnemonic trick. For example, remember ABC-612 by thinking "Another Big Creep" and assigning 6 as the age the driver started school, and 12 as when he probably dropped out. Similarly, the letters in DEF-816 might become "Drunk Every Friday." The numbers could represent "ate" (what you did before the ride) and 16 (the age when you got your license). The meaning doesn't matter, just as long as you can recite the number later for police.

One cyclist, the victim of a hit-and-run, used pebbles to re-create the plate number as he lay by the side of the road. Another method involves carrying a pen and paper in your saddle bag so you can stop and record the number.

If you can file away the plate number while calmly continuing to ride, the harassing motorist will be disappointed. He was looking to anger or upset you. Instead, he got no reaction at all. "What a drag," he says to himself. "These cyclists are no fun at all. Maybe I could get more action downtown scaring pedestrians."

If you ride frequently, harassment is bound to happen. When it does, avoid that first impulse to strike back and take satisfaction in later amends. When reporting such an incident to police, be adamant, since they may be reluctant to pursue the driver if you weren't injured.

If you couldn't see the plate number, give a description (year, make, model, color, distinguishing features) of the car. The more familiar you are with your state's motor vehicle code, the better you'll be able to pinpoint the exact violation, whether harassment, reckless driving, launching a projectile from a moving vehicle, or hit-and-run. If there were witnesses to the offense, try to get their names as well.

Finally, be confident in the understanding that you are denying the driver his jollies, while making the road safer for all cyclists. Just be careful when walking through intersections the next time you're in town.

10 THE FACTS ABOUT CYCLING NUTRITION

In most recreational sports, eating is something you do afterward and, occasionally, beforehand. But in cycling, eating is often an important part of the activity. To most beginning riders, this is news. So, in true journalistic style, here are the pertinent facts—as reporters say, the "why, when, what, and how"—of eating, drinking, and cycling.

Why **you need to eat and drink on the bike.** Food replenishes the energy burned while riding. Every time you eat something, your body takes the food's carbohydrate (a natural compound derived from starches and sugars) and stores it as fuel (glycogen) in your muscles. You have enough stored glycogen to provide energy for short rides. For longer efforts, however, you need to eat or your glycogen stores will become depleted. When this occurs, less fuel reaches your brain and muscles and you feel dizzy and tired. Cyclists call this "bonking."

To avoid the bonk, new riders generally should carry something to eat if they'll be cycling for 90 minutes or longer. In addition, cycling also results in fluid loss. To avoid dehydration and its debilitating effects, never leave home without a full water bottle.

When you should eat and drink. While riding, drink before you're thirsty and eat before you're hungry. If you wait for your body to tell you it needs nourishment, the energy won't be able to reach your muscles fast enough to help. One rule of thumb is to take a big swig from your water bottle every 15 minutes. You should consume about 20 ounces or one standard bottle of liquid per hour (more if it's hot and humid). Another is to allow yourself about an hour for digestion before riding. If you'll be cycling for more than 90 minutes, nibble periodically during the ride. Don't stuff yourself at a mid-ride meal. Your digestive system requires a lot of blood to process such meals, which leaves less for delivering oxygen to your muscles.

What you should eat and drink. Here are six suggestions.

- For fluid replacement on short rides, water is excellent. Commercial sports or energy drinks such as BodyFuel, Exceed, and Max are preferred by many cyclists for longer rides. This is because they replenish lost liquid *and* glycogen stores, and are easier for the body to process than solids. According to studies, cyclists can ride nearly a third farther when ingesting a sports drink.
- When off the bike, your diet should be 60 to 70 percent carbohydrate, 20 to 30 percent protein, and about 10 percent fat. High-carbo foods include fruit, pasta, potatoes, whole-grain breads, and vegetables.
- Perhaps the most popular on-bike food is the banana. It's easy to eat, provides 105 calories from carbohydrate and replaces potassium, an important element lost via sweating. Other fresh fruit such as pears (98 calories) and apples (81 calories) also provides carbohydrates, vitamins, minerals, and water—all necessary fuels for cycling.
- Generally, avoid high-fat treats such as candy while riding. Fat is an ineffective fuel source compared to carbohydrates. Researchers report that when you're burning fat for energy, you can reach only 50 to 60 percent of your aerobic potential.
- Many long-distance cyclists mix nuts, raisins, whole-grain or enriched cereal, and other favorites into a personalized concoction called gorp. This delivers a steady flow of carbohydrates and is easy to nibble.

- Caffeine (coffee, cola, tea) may give you a momentary boost, but it also encourages fluid loss through urination. Since riding itself reduces fluid levels, heavy caffeine intake is not recommended. In any case, research shows caffeine's uplifting effects decrease once you become a routine user.

How **to eat while riding.** The best place to store food while riding is in the rear pockets of your jersey. To reach it, first grip the handlebar with one hand near the stem to hold the bike steady. Then reach around with the other hand to grab that banana, which you can peel with your teeth and eat. Another approach is to snack during rest stops. It's common for cyclists to stash food in seat or handlebar bags for devouring at spontaneous roadside picnics.

Finally, don't forget the postride meal. As a cyclist, you'll regularly burn hundreds if not thousands of calories while exercising. So when you get home, you can guiltlessly enjoy an extra helping of your favorite food—and that's the best news of all.

11 FAST FOODS

Nutritionists write books on the subject. Researchers conduct long, extensive studies. Magazines publish monthly columns. But in the end, sports nutrition often comes down to this: pacing the aisles of a 7-Eleven or perusing the menu board at McDonald's when you're halfway through a ride and hungry. If you can make the right choices in these situations, you may know all that's necessary about cycling nutrition.

The first thing to realize is the value of carbohydrate. As explained previously, this is your body's most effective fuel for exercise. Foods that offer a high percentage of carbohydrate are digested faster and used more efficiently than foods that are high in fat or protein. The ideal cycling food should be at least 55 percent carbohydrate and no more than 30 percent fat. With this in mind, let's take a stroll through a convenience store to evaluate some typical choices. Afterward, we'll stop at a fast-food restaurant to learn the best (and worst) selections there. Remember that these foods are not necessarily the most nutritious choices for cycling, but rather the best of the available evils.

Aisle 1: Snack items. A 2-ounce bag of Lay's potato chips offers 306 calories, but 58 percent come from fat. By comparison, a bag of tortilla chips has about the same number of total calories, but only 42 percent are from fat—better than potato chips but still not low enough.

Nuts and seeds are even worse. Split a 6-ounce can of peanuts with your riding partner and you'll each get 471 calories. A whopping 77 percent of these are fat calories, while only 13 percent are carbohydrate. Likewise, a half can of almonds translates into 270 calories, of which 80 percent are fat and 13 percent are carbohydrate. And of the 314 calories in a 2-ounce pouch of sunflower seeds, 76 percent are fat and 14 percent are carbohydrate.

Here, the best choice is a bag of pretzels. Unlike nuts and seeds, they aren't naturally high in fat. And unlike chips, they aren't fried. If you eat half of a 10-ounce bag of Rold Gold pretzel sticks (salt-free, if possible), you'll get 550 calories, of which 81 percent are carbohydrate and only 6 percent are fat.

Aisle 2: Cookies. On a long ride you can easily burn 3,000 to 5,000 calories. Thus, you need high-calorie replenishment. Cookies provide plenty of calories, but they're often the wrong kind. For instance, two Pepperidge Farm chocolate chip cookies supply about 320 calories, but 41 percent are from fat. Two oatmeal cookies give about 300 calories, of which 38 percent are fat.

Fig bars are the wisest selection in this aisle. Two give you 106 calories—83 percent from carbohydrate and just 17 percent from fat. Since their calorie content is about a third lower than that of most cookies, you can have three times as many. This allows you to satisfy your hunger during a ride.

Aisle 3: Candy bars. As part of an everyday diet, candy bars and other "junk" foods are a bad idea. Besides being fattening, they offer few nutrients.

However, during a ride, sugary foods can play an important role by providing a quick shot of carbohydrate. The trick is to get this boost without also getting a large dose of fat. This isn't easy. A Snickers bar (270 calories) contains about an equal proportion of fat and carbohydrate. The same can be said for most candy bars, except Milky Way. Of its 260 calories, 66 percent come from carbohydrate and 31 percent from fat.

Aisle 4: Pastry. Because of their creams and fillings, most pastry items provide more fat than carbohydrate. For instance, a Hostess cake doughnut (115 calories) is 55 percent fat.

Believe it or not, the best choice in this category may be that old junk food standard, Twinkies. That's right, two of them provide 286 calories—68 percent from carbohydrate and only 26 percent from fat.

Aisle 5: Ice cream and yogurt. While regular ice cream is extremely high in fat, some related products make pretty good cycling fuel. Of the 167 calories in an ice-cream sandwich, for instance, nearly two-thirds come from carbohydrate and only a third from fat. A Popsicle's even better. All of its 65 calories come from sugar, which is a form of carbohydrate.

But the best selection in the dairy case is yogurt. A cup of fruit-flavored low-fat yogurt (225 calories) is 75 percent carbohydrate and only 10 percent fat. And unlike ice-cream sandwiches and Popsicles, yogurt is nutritious, providing more calcium and B vitamins.

Aisle 6: Cold drinks. It's easy to find high-carbohydrate sources in this area. Twelve ounces of soda supply 140 to 180 calories, all of which are carbohydrate from sugar. A more nutritious alternative that's also 100 percent carbohydrate is fruit juice (180 calories per 12 ounces). But the best choice is Gatorade. Besides being totally carbohydrate, it replaces potassium and other elements lost in sweat, and is designed to reach your bloodstream quickly.

Aisle 7: Fruit. If you find a convenience store or corner market with fresh fruit, go for it. Fruit is nearly 100 percent carbohydrate and a good source of vitamins, minerals, and fiber. A banana provides 105 calories, an apple about 80, and an orange about 60. For endurance and nutrition, this is your best option.

The big board. Most cyclists know that fast food is generally high in fat and low in nutrients. However, a fast-food restaurant is often the most convenient place to eat during a ride. So is it possible to refuel properly under the golden arches or at the home of the Whopper?

The answer is yes. One way is by avoiding the big-name burger. A McDonald's Big Mac, for instance, packs 563 calories—53 percent from fat and only 28 percent from carbohydrate. In addition, avoid french fries. A regular order adds 220 calories, of which half are fat. A chocolate shake isn't as bad (383 calories, 21 percent fat). But a burger, fries, and a shake total 1,150 calories—a meal that's almost half fat.

A better option is a chicken sandwich with barbecue sauce, 6 ounces of orange juice, and a carton of low-fat milk. This gives you about 625 calories—more than half from carbohydrate and only 25 percent from fat.

The best type of fast food can be found at Italian or Mexican outlets. Four slices of a 12-inch cheese pizza (653 calories) are 59 percent carbohydrate and just 17 percent fat. Likewise, at Taco Bell, a bean tostada (179 calories), an order of beans and cheese (232 calories), or a bean burrito (350 calories) are each more than 50 percent carbohydrate and less than 30 percent fat—not quite as good as Twinkies, but a fine midride meal nonetheless.

12 PERFECT YOUR RIDING POSITION

Take any European pro cyclist. Replace his bright team jersey with a T-shirt, disguise his rippling leg muscles with hair and knee socks, plop a hardshell helmet on his head, and put him on his bike in the midst of a rolling gaggle of Sunday tourists.

He'll still stick out like a Colnago in K-Mart because his grace, fluidity, and economy of motion (what the French call *souplesse*) make it seem as if he were born on his bike.

Actually, it's the other way around. His bicycle is set up to maximize his comfort and efficiency. Each adjustment conforms to his body dimensions and riding style. Admittedly, it takes years of experience and thousands of miles to develop the flawless form of a pro. But the first—and most important—step toward that lofty goal is to make your bicycle fit as if it were custom built. We'll examine various simple and effective ways to do this.

Before we begin, be certain your bike is the correct size. Refer to chapter 3 or make this quick check: Wearing your riding shoes, straddle your bike and measure the distance between your crotch and the top tube. If it's between 1 and 2 inches, you're on the money. If you're outside this range and find it impossible to make some of the following adjustments, consider replacing your bike with one that fits. (Note: This sizing and adjustment information doesn't apply to a mountain bike, which should be about 2 to 3 inches smaller than your road bike.)

Do the following procedures in the order they're discussed.

Foot Position

Perfect riding position starts with the feet. These are the points through which your energy is transferred to the bicycle. Improper foot position makes you a less efficient pedaler and stresses the knees.

Contrary to the belief of many beginners, pedals aren't supposed to nestle in the arch of the foot. They belong under the ball of the foot. This promotes the agility to spin and brings the calf muscles into play, allowing you to press down when you want extra power.

Most recreational cyclists should position the ball of each foot directly over the pedal axle. Exceptions are high-cadence spinners, who benefit from having their feet about ¼ inch rearward, and heavily muscled big-gear mashers, whose powerful quadriceps tend to overstress their Achilles tendons and calves unless their feet are farther into the pedals.

If you ride without toe clips it will be difficult to keep your feet properly positioned. Identify the center of the balls of your feet by making a mark on the outside of each shoe, then glance down occasionally to make sure the marks are in line with the pedal axle.

Toe clips are recommended because they help maintain proper foot position and increase pedaling efficiency. When the ball of your foot is over the pedal axle, the toe of your shoe should be about ⅛ inch from the end of the clip. This space is necessary to prevent pressure on your toes and damage to the end of your shoes. If your foot size is between clip sizes, you can either use the larger size and have extra room, or select the smaller size and place washers between the pedals and clips to gain the necessary space.

If you wear cleated cycling shoes, foot-over-pedal position becomes a function of cleat location. To find the balls of your feet through rigid-sole cycling shoes, Bill Farrell, developer of the Fit Kit sizing system, recommends painting a white dot on the ball of your right foot, then carefully pressing the foot to the sole of the left shoe (cleat removed) to transfer the paint. Do the same with the left foot and right shoe. Next, double-check by drilling a small hole through the dot on each sole. Put the shoes on and poke a paint-dipped spoke through the holes. These new dots should appear directly on the ball of each foot. Attach the cleats so that when the shoes are engaged with the pedals, the sole holes are over the center of the pedal axles.

Rotational alignment of the cleats is critical, too. An unnatural foot position during pedaling will often result in knee injury. Simply positioning the feet straight ahead will work for some riders, but it's best to ride a few miles with the cleats loose enough to let your feet find their natural alignment. It's not uncommon for them to be at different angles. Then have a friend reach under and tighten the cleats before you dismount. (If knee problems develop despite attempts to correctly adjust your cleats and overall riding position, visit a bike shop that uses the Fit Kit and its Rotational Adjustment Device, a cleat-positioning tool.)

Saddle Tilt

Before adjusting the saddle height or fore/aft position, make sure its top is level (or nearly so) with the ground. Tilt it *slightly* up or down only if doing so is necessary for comfort. Generally, it's risky to point the nose down because it can cause arm fatigue as you resist the tendency to slide forward.

Try riding no-hands or with very light pressure on the handlebar. If you slide forward, tilt the nose of the saddle up slightly. Go easy, because a high nose can cause crotch discomfort and numbness when you lean into the handlebar. Also, too much upward tilt will cause you to slide off the rear as you push hard on climbs.

To check saddle tilt, lay a broom or yardstick lengthwise on top and see how it relates to the frame's top tube. If you have a saddle that kicks up in the rear, adjust it with the yardstick pointing down a few degrees in front, which makes the sitting area level. (See photograph 2-1.)

Photograph 2-1. Use a straightedge to check saddle angle. Start with the saddle parallel to the ground (or top tube, if you're sure it doesn't slope). Tilt the nose up slightly if this improves comfort.

Saddle Height

The effort it takes to ride a bike is profoundly influenced by saddle height. Studies have shown that pedaling efficiency falls off rapidly if the saddle is even slightly too low or too high.

Efficiency isn't the same as power. Although the human leg can exert the most force when almost straight, pedaling a bicycle with the seat raised to such a height is unstable, inefficient, and can promote knee trouble. It is better to use a lower saddle and slide back to increase the distance to the pedals when you want more power. Good riders do this instinctively as they crank up steep grades or push in their top gear. Racing saddles with a rear "spoiler" aid this effort by lifting the body even higher and providing a lip to push against.

A saddle that's too low squanders both efficiency and power. It prevents full use of the thigh muscles, yielding a poor return for the energy expended.

Saddle height is directly related to inseam length–the longer the leg, the higher the saddle. Although every coach and framebuilder has a pet formula, one of the oldest still works well for the majority of riders. With your bare feet 6 inches apart, hold a tape measure firmly into your crotch and measure to the floor. (Have a friend help so you're exact.) Multiply this number by 1.09, then use the result to set the distance from the top of the saddle to the center of the pedal axle when the crankarm is in line with the seat tube.

Another popular method is to pedal backward using your heels. Raise the saddle to just below the point where you must rock your hips to keep your feet in contact. This method usually locates the saddle several millimeters lower than the 1.09 formula. A saddle height between these two extremes will work well for almost every rider.

Of course, foot length, pedaling style, and crankarm length all affect saddle height. For example, someone who pedals with toes pointed downward will need a slightly higher saddle than a rider of the same inseam length who pedals flat-footed. And if the feet of the toes-down pedaler happen to be long in proportion to inseam length, the saddle must be even higher. If you think it's necessary to alter your basic saddle height to accommodate such variables, do it in small increments. And always record your initial measurements so you can return to your original position if things go awry.

These aberrations, along with esoterica such as sole thickness and pedal cage height, are why saddle height is not an exact science. Our recommendations will put you within a centimeter of your ideal. Then take your body's advice (if any) and make slight adjustments. Finally, you will have to alter your saddle height occasionally if you are still growing or ride year-round. It should be lowered in winter in proportion to the thickness of extra layers of tights and shorts, or if cold weather makes your leg muscles less supple.

Knee-to-Pedal Relationship

The rails under a saddle allow it to be moved forward or backward about 2 inches. This adjustment is not intended for, nor should it be used for, fine-tuning your reach to the handlebar, which is accomplished with the stem extension. The only reason a saddle's fore/aft location should be changed is to put the rider in a more efficient position over the pedals. Here's how this is done: First, locate each leg's tibial tuberosity—the bony bump below the kneecap. This conveniently lies on a vertical line that passes through the center of the knee joint when the crankarm is directly forward (3 o'clock). This vertical line should also bisect the pedal axle.

To see if it does, sit in the center of the saddle as when riding. (It's helpful if the bike is mounted on a resistance trainer, but be certain the top tube is level with the floor.) Turn one crankarm to the 3 o'clock position, then drop a plumb line (a nut on a string will do) from the front of your tibial tuberosity. Angle your knee slightly outward and see where the string passes the pedal axle. (See photograph 2-2.) Slide on the saddle until the string and axle line up, then dismount and move the saddle accordingly. Repeat until you get it right. You're establishing your normal riding position, from which you can scoot forward to increase your spin or slide back to power up a hill.

A midsize bike with a typical seat angle of 73.5 degrees allows sufficient fore/aft saddle adjustment to accommodate most riders. But a racing bike with a steep 75-degree seat angle—the current fashion—may not allow a long-thighed rider to put the seat back far enough. By its design, such a bike places the seat about an inch farther forward than the previous example.

Short women on stock bikes may have difficulty with this adjustment for two related reasons. First, women typically

Photograph 2-2. A plumb line dropped from the center of the knee-cap (using the tibial tuberosity to locate this point) should bisect the pedal spindle when the crankarm is at 3 o'clock.

have longer femurs than men of the same height, but most frames are designed for the average male's body proportions. Second, small frames often have steep seat angles in order to shorten the top tube for a more comfortable reach to the handlebar. This dilemma is a reason some progressive bike manufacturers have introduced models specifically designed for women.

Reach to Handlebar

If you're with us so far, your riding position from the waist down should be indistinguishable from that of a world champion. But saddle adjustments are simple compared to the variables of proper handlebar position.

The dimension that most affects upper body position is reach, the combined measurement of the top tube and handlebar stem extension. On a mass-produced frame, the length of the top tube (measured from the center of the seat tube to the center of the head tube) is proportional to the frame size (i.e., the seat tube length) and corresponds to the upper body measurements of the average cyclist who would need that size frame. As mentioned, only recently have manufacturers begun addressing the needs of female cyclists, who typically have longer legs and shorter torsos than men of the same height.

Stems come in forward extensions of 4 to 14 cm to permit fine-tuning a bicycle to its rider. The problem comes in deciding whose sizing method to use. Of several common systems, however, one seems to work well in almost every case.

Begin by putting the top of the handlebar 1 inch lower than the top of the saddle. This height will be fine for most riders, although some with supple backs and a concern for aerodynamics may prefer the stem slightly lower. Others may find it more comfortable to put the handlebar at saddle height. Never exceed the stem's "max-height" line; 2 inches must remain in the steerer tube or it could be deformed by the expander plug.

The brake levers should be placed so the bottom of each lever lines up with the bottom edge of the handlebar, assuming this edge is within about 10 degrees of horizontal. Those whose have a handlebar with a deep drop, such as the Cinelli 66, may want to position the levers higher on the curve. The exact tilt of the handlebar is up to you. Many racers like the bottom perfectly horizontal for a good grip when sprinting. Others find more hand comfort when the bar is pointing midway between the seat lug and the rear wheel axle. Any more tilt than this will exceed 10 degrees.

Now check for proper stem extension. Get on the bike and assume a normal riding position with hands on the drops of the handlebar and elbows slightly bent. Have a friend hold a plumb line to the end of your nose. (See photograph 2-3.) It should fall about 1 inch behind the handlebar. This method works with racing and touring bikes because it's not keyed to the frame's front-end geometry. If the plumb line misses the mark by much, you can estimate what size the replacement stem should be.

Another popular method is to assume the same riding

position and look down at the front hub. If you can't see it because the handlebar is in the way, the stem extension is correct. This method considers torso length and back flexibility, but it only works on a racing bike with a 73- or 74-degree head angle and complementary fork rake. On a touring bike, the front wheel will be farther forward.

Photograph 2-3. On a bike with an ideal reach (top tube plus stem extension), a plumb line from your nose should fall about an inch behind the handlebar when you're sitting with hands on the drops and elbows slightly bent. In this position on a racing bike, the handlebar should block your view of the front hub.

Give It Time

After you've carefully made all these adjustments, minor aches and pains may develop before your body adapts to its new riding posture. This is normal, so resist the temptation to fiddle with your position. You'll become accustomed to it after a few rides, and your cycling performance will improve. Then you can concentrate on your bike-handling skills and fitness, confident that your riding position is as good as can be.

13 SMART SHIFTING

The quickest, easiest way to become a better rider is to learn how to shift gears efficiently. This may seem obvious, especially since the invention of index drivetrains, which make shifting as easy as pushing the buttons on a car radio. But many riders still don't understand the mechanics of their gear systems, and thus don't take full advantage of them.

So here are the basics, along with tips on such techniques as double shifting and avoiding noisy cross-chain gears. You'll even learn how to design a gear chart and devise your most efficient shifting pattern.

Shifting Basics

A 12-speed road bike has two front chainrings and six rear freewheel cogs. Do most of your shifting on the rear (using the right shift lever). The steps, or size differences, between cogs are smaller than the steps between chainrings, enabling you to make small adjustments in your gearing as the terrain changes slightly. (A recreational rider's goal should be to maintain a pedaling cadence of 75 to 90 revolutions per minute.) Also, rear shifts are faster and easier than switching chainrings (done with the left lever).

You may find it best to use the left hand for the left lever and the right hand for the right lever. Others prefer to do all their shifting with the right hand. For most level and uphill riding, use the small inner chainring. Change to the big outer ring when descending or riding with a tail wind.

Here's another way to know when to shift chainrings. Starting with the lowest gear (smallest ring/biggest cog), push the right lever forward to get higher gears. If the right lever is as far forward as it will go but you still need a higher gear, use the left lever to cross over to the big chainring (hence, the name "crossover" gearing). Similarly, when you run out of lower gears while using the big chainring, cross over to the small ring.

The same principles apply to mountain bikes, but most have three chainrings instead of two. Use the middle ring for most of your riding, on- or off-road. Cross over from the middle to the outer ring when you run out of higher gears. Cross over from the middle to the inner ring when you run out of lower gears.

As you ride, keep in mind that the drivetrain should be relatively noise-free. If, after shifting cogs, you hear a scraping sound coming from the front derailleur, move the left lever in the opposite direction that you moved the right (without actually changing chainrings). The noise should go away.

If your bike has index "click" shifting and you hear a rattling noise from the rear derailleur, you may need to adjust the cable tension. This can be easily done by using the barrel adjuster where the cable enters the derailleur. If you have the same problem with a nonindex ("friction") system, simply move the right shift lever slightly until the noise goes away.

Double Shifting

Here's an embellishment on the basic crossover technique. When switching chainrings, the resulting change may be more than you want. In this case, move the right lever in the same direction that you moved the left until you've shifted one or two cogs. Moving both levers at nearly the same time is called "double shifting." It isn't necessary to move the two levers simultaneously. Simply move one lever, then the other.

Riders of 22-inch or larger frames should use their right hand for double shifts. Those with smaller bikes or frames with oversize tubing may have trouble reaching the left lever. In this case, use the left hand for that lever.

Always try to anticipate front shifts. Look at the road or trail ahead. If there's a hill, change to the small ring even if it requires a double shift. This way, when the hill steepens, you can move to an even lower gear with a quick rear shift. Switching chainrings when you're pushing hard in the middle of a climb is difficult and may make your drivetrain malfunction.

Cross-Chain Gears

There are certain gear combinations you should avoid. Those that result in chain "deflection" cause friction and noise. This is most pronounced when the chain is on the outer ring and the innermost cog, or on the inner ring and the outermost cog. (See illustration 2-2.) These "big-to-big" and "small-to-small" combinations are known as the cross-chain gears.

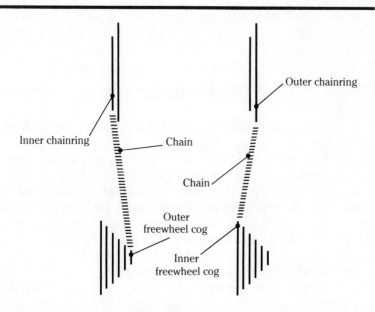

Illustration 2-2. Cross-chain gears. You should avoid using these gears because the resulting chain deflection will cause friction and noise.

To bypass these gears on a road bike, cross over to the other chainring one shift early. If you are on the outer ring and the second-largest cog—but you still need a lower gear—switch rings rather than shift to the largest cog.

Similarly, if you are on the inner ring and the second-smallest cog but still need a higher gear, cross over to the outer ring rather than shift to the smallest cog.

Mountain bikes are a bit different. When riding in the middle ring, it's okay to use any of the cogs because chain deflection is minimal. Deflection is more pronounced with the outer ring, so most riders use only the three smallest cogs with it. Likewise, the inner ring is used with only the three largest cogs. This keeps the chain from hanging slack or rubbing against the front derailleur or the middle ring. In addition, using the inner ring with the three smallest cogs usually duplicates gears that you could achieve using the middle ring.

Don't worry if you accidentally shift into the cross-chain gears—it won't hurt your bike unless the chain is too short to accommodate the "big-to-big" combination and you try to force the shift.

A Graduate Course

This information will get you started right. But to learn more about your gearing, you need to calculate each chainring and cog combination in inches and plot the results on a chart.

Start by determining the number of teeth on each chainring and cog. (Chainrings are usually stamped with the number of teeth, but you'll probably need to count the teeth on your cogs.) Use a gear table to determine each combination in inches. This is the universal way of referring to bicycle gear ratios. It's based on the number of chainring and freewheel teeth, and the diameter of the rear wheel.

If you don't have a gear table, use this formula: Divide the number of teeth on the chainring by the number of teeth on the cog, and multiply by the wheel diameter in inches (27 inches for road bikes, 26 for mountain bikes). Thus, a road bike with a 52-tooth outer ring and a 13T outer cog would have a high gear of 108 inches (52 divided by 13, multiplied by 27).

This is considered a "big" gear and is usually reserved for pedaling downhill at 30 mph. A low number such as 45 inches is a good gear for climbing.

Plot your gears on a chart with the cogs on the left and the chainrings at the top. Fill in the number of inches for each chainring/cog combination. The value of such a chart is in determining a shifting sequence. Ideally, the steps between gears (in inches) should be small and the sequence should be easy to remember. (It might help to tape a small version of your chart to your handlebar until you learn the shifting pattern.)

Most moderately priced road bikes have 52- and 42-tooth chainrings. Mountain bikes in this price range have 48/38/28T chainrings. But the freewheels vary considerably. Road bike freewheels have two basic arrangements (and corresponding shifting sequences)—alpine and crossover. Alpine freewheels have a nearly uniform 15 percent change between cogs. A typical alpine freewheel might be 14-16-18-21-24-28T. Crossover freewheels have closer steps between the small cogs (since these cogs are used most often) and wider steps between the large cogs. A typical crossover freewheel might be 14-15-17-20-23-28T.

Illustration 2-3 shows how the shifting patterns differ for the two arrangements. Notice that the shifting sequence (indicated by arrows) does not follow the progression of gear inches exactly. For the crossover road bike, for instance, the lowest gear is 41 inches (42T chainring with a 28T cog, designated as 42×28). To get the smallest possible increase in gear inches, you would shift to 42×23 (49 inches), then to 52×28 (50 inches), then to 42×20 (57 inches), then to 52×23 (61 inches), and so on. But this sequence would result in cross-chain gears and an impossibly complicated shifting pattern. Instead, crossover and alpine setups sacrifice some gears to achieve an easy-to-remember sequence. (There are about eight commonly used gears on a crossover road bike, and ten on a crossover mountain bike.)

Notice that alpine gearing requires frequent double shifts to hit all the intermediate gears. You can shift an alpine like a crossover, but you'll notice the larger steps between cogs.

What if you don't like your gearing arrangement? Maybe your high isn't high enough, or your low isn't low enough. All is not lost. Different cogs are readily available. It's also possible to switch chainrings or add a third chainring. To learn more, consult our book *Bicycling Magazine's Complete Guide to Upgrading Your Bike*.

		Chainrings	
		42T	**52T**
Freewheel cogs	14	(81)	• 8th **100**
	15	76 5th •	• 7th 94
	17	67 4th •	• 6th 83
	20	57 3rd •	70
	23	49 2nd •	61
	28	41 1st •	(50)

CROSSOVER
Road Bike

		Chainrings	
		42T	**52T**
Freewheel cogs	14	(81) 9th •	• 11th **100**
	16	71 7th •	• 10th 88
	18	63 5th •	• 8th 78
	21	54 3rd •	• 6th 67
	24	47 2nd •	• 4th 59
	28	41 1st •	(50)

ALPINE
Road Bike

		Chainrings		
		28T	**38T**	**48T**
Freewheel cogs	14	(52)	8th • 71	• 10th 89
	15	(49)	7th • 66	• 9th 83
	17	(43)	6th • 58	73
	20	36	5th • 49	62
	23	32 2nd •	4th • 43	(54)
	28	26 1st •	3rd • 35	(45)

CROSSOVER
Mountain Bike

Illustration 2-3. Shifting patterns.

■14■ BASIC BIKE CARE

Plenty of mechanical problems can be avoided with just a little know-how and a few minutes of maintenance. When a novice cyclist brings a malfunctioning bike into a shop for service, it's usually due to one of the following five problems. Here are some straightforward tips for preventing and remedying each of them.

Damaged Wheels

Pneumatic (air-filled) inner tubes and tires roll well, cushion the ride, and protect the rims from damage. But even perfectly good inner tubes gradually lose air through microscopic pores in the rubber. A high-performance butyl inner tube, for instance, can lose 30 percent of its pressure in a month.

Preventing underinflation problems such as poor tire performance, pinch flats, and damaged rims is simply a matter of inflating the tires to their recommended pressure (written on the sidewall) once a week. Another good precaution is to squeeze each tire between your thumb and index finger before every ride to determine if they've lost pressure due to a puncture.

Fat, low-pressure tires, such as those on mountain bikes, require filling less often. Once a month should do. But use the pinch test before each ride to check for leaks.

Knowing how to operate your tire valves will make proper inflation easier. There are two types of valves used on bicycle tires: Presta and Schrader. Presta valves, also known as needle or French valves, are metal except for their seals. They can contain higher pressures than Schrader valves and are used mostly on high-performance road bike tubes. Before adding or releasing air, the top of the valve must be unscrewed. After the tire is filled, it must be tightened.

Schrader valves are the same as those on cars. But don't use a service station air pump to fill them. Such pumps are designed to fill higher volume tires quickly and can burst a bicycle tube.

Frame-fit and floor pumps for both types of valves are

sold in bike shops. Some pumps are reversible and can fit either type of valve. Adapters that let a Presta valve accept air from a Schrader pump are also available.

Another part of the wheel that many beginners neglect is the quick-release mechanism. It's operated by the lever and hand-turned nut located at the front and rear axle. It's important because it secures the wheels to the frame. If it's open or loose, a serious crash can result. Quick-releases are used instead of bolts to make wheel removal more convenient.

Correct use of the front quick-release involves placing the wheel into the dropouts (ends of the fork) as far as it will go. Next, tighten the quick-release by pushing the lever back until it's in the closed position. (Most new levers are marked "open" and "closed.") The lever should rest in line with the fork blade or trail behind it. The squeezing force of the quick-release can be adjusted by turning the nut opposite the lever. The lever should provide firm resistance as it is closed—enough to briefly imprint the palm of your hand. (Some bikes have fork dropout retainers that require unscrewing the quick-release nut to remove the wheel.)

The procedure is the same for the rear wheel, except for the additional step of making sure the wheel is aligned with the seat tube (the frame member directly in front of the wheel). Also, index shifting systems work best when the axle is positioned near the front of the dropout slots. Before the quick-release is tightened, the rear wheel can be positioned fore and aft and centered with small, built-in adjuster screws located at the rear of the dropouts.

Practice using the quick-releases, and have an experienced cyclist check your work.

Lack of Lubrication

There are plenty of moving parts on a bicycle, and many are exposed to road grit. Thus, they require occasional lubrication to keep them working properly. Bike shops sell a variety of spray and drip lubes.

Spray lubes usually come with a small plastic tube that attaches to the nozzle. This allows the spray to be directed where you want it. Drip lubes are even more precise. They come in small bottles and permit lube application one drop at a time. Many experienced cyclists favor the latter.

A road bike chain needs lubrication about once every 300 miles; a mountain bike chain, every ride or two, depending on conditions. A light coat is best because any excess will attract dirt and splash on the wheel and frame. To lube the chain, place the bike where you can freely turn the pedals backward. Put a rag over the lower part of the rear rim to keep it clean. Hold the nozzle near the chain, slowly spin the crank, and apply the lubricant as the chain passes over the top pulley of the rear derailleur. After you've done the entire chain, hold a lint-free rag loosely around it and spin the crank backward to remove excess lube and grit. It's best to do this job 24 hours before riding. This will allow the lube's liquid carrier to fully evaporate and thereby keep things cleaner.

The pivot points—where moving parts meet—need occasional lubrication, too. The front and rear derailleur pivots are examples, as are brake arms and levers. (Don't get lube on the brake pads, though.) If these parts get dry and gritty they may stick.

Modern cables and casings require less care than their predecessors, but an occasional drop of oil where the cable enters the casing, and at the cable guides under the bottom bracket, will keep them moving smoothly.

Loose Nuts and Bolts

Many problems are caused by a bolt or nut that worked loose or dropped off because of road vibration. This often happens to water bottle cages, racks, toe clips, and other attachments.

Check bolt and nut tightness a few times each season. Use a set of Allen and metric wrenches (available at bike shops) to make sure every one is snug. Be sure to check:

- Handlebar and stem (6mm Allen or adjustable wrench)
- Wheel nuts, if any (15mm Allen or adjustable wrench)
- Chainring bolts (5mm Allen wrench)
- Crankarm bolts (screwdriver or 5mm Allen wrench to

remove dust cap; special 14 or 15mm socket wrench
for bolts)
- Accessories and hardware (screwdriver, adjustable
wrenches, Allen wrenches)

Caution: Do not overtighten, because most nuts and bolts
are small. Their threads can easily be damaged if force is used.

Stretched Cables

New cables will stretch until they reach a stable length.
When this happens, the components they operate often come
out of adjustment. For example, index derailleurs shift poorly
when cables are loose. If you buy a new bike, your shop will
readjust cables during a follow-up check (usually free).

To help riders keep things working properly, manufacturers provide adjuster barrels. These are small threaded fittings
on the brakes and rear derailleur that permit cable tension
adjustment without tools. Turning them counterclockwise adds
tension, tightening your brakes or taking slack out of the
derailleur cable.

Marred Finish

Rust and corrosion are enemies of any metal object. If left
outside, your bicycle will eventually deteriorate. The first precaution is to store your bike indoors. Use a vinyl-coated hook
to hang it from one wheel in a corner of the garage or basement.
Apartment dwellers can buy attractive wall or floor racks for
bike storage.

Better bikes are well protected from corrosion with quality paint jobs, chrome plating, and aluminum anodizing. These
finishes can be made even more durable with a coat of wax.
Shops carry brands made especially for bikes.

Handle your bike carefully to avoid chipping the paint.
Don't lean it against the frame, and be careful when placing it

on a car rack or in a trunk. If you do chip the paint, touch it up as soon as possible. If your bike shop doesn't have the right color, try an automotive store or hobby shop.

Finally, don't hesitate to ask your bike dealer for an explanation or demonstration of any aspect of basic bike maintenance. Most dealers pride themselves on service and will gladly invest the time required to keep you happy.

15 FIXING A FLAT

A flat tire is one of those givens in life that occurs at the worst possible moment. To minimize its effect, either never ride farther than you'd care to walk, hone your hitchhiking skills, or learn to repair tires. Assuming you choose the latter, here's a primer for rounding out flats.

Repair kit. Since patching tires with highway tar is virtually impossible, it's important to carry a repair kit. It should include:

- A spare tube (sized to your tire)
- Two or three tire levers
- A patch kit (for the inevitable second puncture)
- A frame-mounted pump

The pump should have either a Schrader or a Presta valve to match your tubes and spare. If you're unsure which type you have, check with your local bike shop.

Removal and inspection. To repair a flat, first find a safe place to work away from traffic. Avoid flipping the bike on its saddle and handlebar, because you might damage the brake cables or replace the wheel improperly. Rather, remove the wounded wheel, lay the bike on its left (nondrivetrain) side, and follow these steps.

1. Deflate the tube completely by depressing the spring-loaded center pin on a Schrader valve, or by partially unscrewing and depressing the pin on a Presta valve.

2. Insert the flat, spoonlike surface of one tire lever between the tire bead and the rim, about 2 inches from the valve. Pry off the bead by pulling the lever toward the hub and hooking it to a spoke. (See illustration 2-4.)

3. Insert a second lever under the same bead about 2 inches to the other side of the valve. Pull the lever down, prying off more of the bead. If the bead is still tight, hook this lever to a spoke and insert a third lever 2 inches farther along the rim. Then pry at 4-inch intervals until the entire bead is free. It's unnecessary to unseat the other bead from the rim to remove the tube.

4. Starting opposite the valve, pull the inner tube from the tire. Then, carefully remove the valve from the rim.

5. Locate the puncture by inflating the tube and listening for a hiss. Water or saliva rubbed on the leak will bubble.

6. Match the damaged part of the tube to the corresponding section of tire to find the cause of the puncture. Inspect the tire for holes, cut threads, or a detached bead. You might find a shard of glass or other sharp object lodged in the tread.

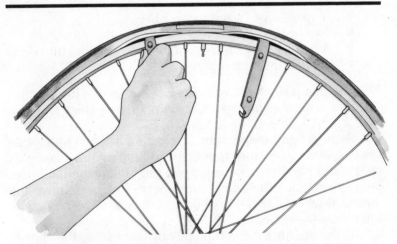

Illustration 2-4. Using a tire lever to remove the tire bead.

Remove all foreign matter and double-check by feeling under the tread. If the tire has a hole larger than ⅛ inch, you must repair it to contain the tube. A folded dollar bill works well in an emergency (it's linen, not paper). Just place it across the hole before installing the tube. Inflate only to 75 percent of recommended pressure.

Repairing the tube. On the road, it's easier to install a spare, but if you have to repair the tube, follow these steps.

1. Choose the right patch. Small, round ones work best on pinhole punctures, while long, oval patches fit the dual snake-bite holes made by a rim pinch. Blowouts of ½ inch or more are usually beyond repair.

2. Buff the area around the puncture with sandpaper. Make it slightly larger than the patch.

3. Apply a thin, even coat of glue to the buffed surface and allow it to dry (it will turn from shiny to dull).

4. Peel the backing from the patch and apply it carefully to the glued area, pressing it firmly in place (you only get one chance). Some patches have foil on one side and plastic on the other. The surface under the foil goes against the glue.

Reinstallation. To install the new or repaired tube, follow these steps.

1. Inflate the tube until it just takes shape.

2. Insert the valve into the rim.

3. Carefully work the tube into the tire so there are no kinks or wrinkles.

4. Begin working the bead onto the rim, starting at the valve. Don't use tire levers for installation—you're likely to cause another puncture by pinching the tube.

5. As the bead becomes harder to push onto the rim, deflate the tube completely to provide maximum slack. Then, use the palms of your hands to push the bead into place. (See illustration 2-5.)

6. Fully inflate the tire. Push the valve stem into the tire to ensure that the bead is seated, then pull out firmly and spin the wheel in your hands as you watch the bead line on each side. It should appear just above the rim. If it bulges up or dips below, deflate the tube and use your hands to work the tire into place.

It's best to practice this procedure at home so your road-side repairs will be quick and competent.

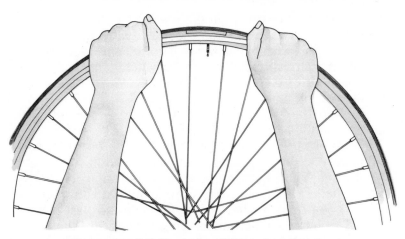

Illustration 2-5. Replacing the bead on the rim.

Part Three

FIRST TOUR, FIRST CENTURY, FIRST RACE

◼16 SETTING GOALS

Cycling is a time-consuming sport. Nevertheless, there are many successful cyclists who work full time, raise families, and otherwise cope with the hassles of everyday life. You won't improve unless you develop similar commitment, dedication, and drive.

"What happens to so many riders is they get excited and are really gung ho in the beginning," says Greg Demgen, 1983 national road champion. "But as time goes by they exhaust their energy and enthusiasm."

To steadily improve and avoid burnout, set specific goals for your first season. But before you can determine what you want to accomplish, you must find time to train properly. According to top riders, it isn't that difficult.

"Commute to work by bicycle," says Pete Penseyres, two-time Race Across America (RAAM) winner and perhaps the ultimate commuter. Every day, he cycles 30 miles each way to his job as a chemistry supervisor at the San Onofre nuclear plant in Southern California. His 90-minute commuting time doesn't differ much from his co-workers'. "The difference is, when they get home they still have to train," says Penseyres, "but I'm done."

With some ingenuity, anyone can find an acceptable commuting route. At first, ride to work once or twice a week, then gradually build to a daily commute. Cycling just 10 miles each way will give you an automatic 100 miles for the week.

Besides enabling you to amass mileage, a daily commute will also give you a standard to measure improvement by. Penseyres, for example, gauges his conditioning by how fast he covers his entire route or sections of it. Certainly, Penseyres's success shows how far you can go when you set goals and creatively structure your time to achieve them.

Now it's your turn. On the following pages, set five specific intermediate goals—each a bit more difficult than the last— and a major season-ending goal. Then set deadlines for achieving each one and do whatever it takes to meet them (suggested goals and time frames are included). Since a goal is just a fantasy until you tell someone, share your plan with friends and family. And if possible, get someone to train with you, because peer pressure can be a powerful motivator.

Goal 1 (March or April)

_____

_____

_____

Suggestion: Ride five times in March and ten times in April. Some can be easy 5- to 10-milers, but once a week ride for at least an hour.

Goal 2 (May)

_____

_____

_____

Suggestion: Ride 50 miles a week.

Goal 3 (June)

_____

_____

_____

Suggestion: Ride 75 miles a week, or 300 to 400 miles for the month. Include a 50-mile ride and a 10-mile time trial in which your average speed is at least 15 mph (40 minutes or less).

Goal 4 (July)

_____

_____

_____

Suggestion: Embark on a two- or three-day minitour of 75 to 150 miles, or take part in an organized ride of similar distance. Consult your local bike shop or club for midsummer events in your area.

Goal 5 (August)

_____

_____

_____

Suggestion: Average 100 miles a week or 400 to 500 miles for the month. Include a 75-mile ride and a 10-mile time trial in which your average speed is at least 18 mph (33 minutes or less).

Major Goal

_____

_____

_____

Suggestion: Complete your first century, or ride 100 miles faster than ever before, or do an extended tour of an interesting region. Whatever your major goal, make it specific, determine it early, and circle the date on your calendar. It's easier to stay focused if you have a distinct target.

17 TRAINING FOR AN EXTENDED TOUR

For many fledgling touring cyclists, the new season awakens a dormant urge to take to the road in search of excitement, adventure, discovery, and companionship. But be careful. Without adequate preparation, you may find what you seek. Consider:

- The *excitement* of realizing your bike handles far differently on a steep descent with 50 pounds in the panniers.
- The *adventure* of grinding unsteadily through deepening twilight toward a distant campsite with legs that already retired for the night.
- The *discovery* well into a planned coast-to-coast ride that your favorite saddle is really quite hard and narrow, your handlebar seems farther away each day, and your gearing is suitable for motor-pacing, not loaded touring.
- The *companionship* of a sympathetic bus driver with whom you share the woes of your aborted tour as you hurtle home, days ahead of schedule.

No sensible person would consider entering the Boston Marathon, or stepping into the English Channel, or touching gloves with Mike Tyson without plenty of preparation for the specific task at hand. Likewise, cyclists embarking on an extended tour (any self-sufficient ride lasting more than two days) should already be reasonably strong and fit. While determination might get you through a weekend tour, a longer trip demands a higher level of fitness if it's to be enjoyed.

To gauge your current status and determine how much training you might need, Bryant Stamford, Ph.D., director of the University of Louisville's exercise physiology lab, recommends a simple test: Well in advance of your departure date, determine the average daily mileage for your tour and see if you can ride this distance two or three times a week.

Dr. Stamford suggests a weekly training schedule that alternates two or three typical touring rides (normal distance and pace) with one or two short, high-intensity workouts. These might include out-of-saddle attacks on hills, periodic flatland sprints, or time trials. One day a week should be reserved for a long ride. This will build even more endurance and accustom you to extended periods in the saddle. Most local clubs hold recreational rides every weekend. These are perfect for augmenting your training, besides being a lot of fun.

If your schedule can't accommodate extra time on the bike, try commuting to work. Or if the weather doesn't cooperate when you do have the time, duplicate these long/easy, short/hard workouts on an indoor resistance trainer.

If the mileage you should be doing is quite a bit more than you're used to, Dr. Stamford suggests gradually working toward your goal. At first, start by increasing your total mileage by 10 percent a week. If your body responds well, try a 15 percent jump the next week. Conversely, if the additional mileage leaves you feeling exhausted, don't be afraid to take a day off or even reduce your weekly training.

If you're more than 30 years old, Dr. Stamford recommends taking a stress test before beginning any event-specific training program, regardless of whether your doctor thinks it's necessary. "He may not be used to dealing with athletes," Dr. Stamford explains. "Training for an event is more rigorous than just deciding to start exercising. The training schedule drives you, instead of you driving the training. It can get pretty tough."

Listen to Your Heart

To make this conditioning program even more effective, arrange the workouts according to your optimum training heart rate. Begin by getting a rough idea of your maximum pulse rate. This is done by subtracting your age from 220 if you're male, or 226 if you're female. Then determine your resting pulse rate. You'll need a clock with a second hand positioned near your bed so you can see it without moving. Upon waking, count your heartbeats for 15 seconds by feeling the pulse at your neck, wrist, or chest. Multiply by four. Do this on several consecutive mornings and average the results to determine your resting pulse rate.

Next find your training threshold by taking 60 percent of your maximum heart rate reserve (MHRR). To calculate this value, simply subtract your resting pulse from your maximum rate, multiply by 0.6, and add your resting pulse rate to the result. For example, a 30-year-old with a resting pulse of 60 has an MHRR of 138 beats per minute ($220 - 30 = 190$; $190 - 60 = 130$; $130 \times 0.6 = 78$; $78 + 60 = 138$).

This is the minimum heart rate this person should maintain during each half-hour (or longer) training session in order to improve aerobic capacity. Of course, the higher the heart rate, the greater the training effect. If 60 percent of MHRR feels too easy, substitute 70 or 75 percent in the formula. As you get fitter, you'll have to really tackle the hills or blaze along on the flats to reach this level. If 75 percent is *still* too easy, forget your plans for a leisurely tour and enter the Race Across America!

While cycling, it's easiest to count your pulse at the carotid artery beside the Adam's apple. Or, invest in a pulse monitor. A less precise method is perceived exertion—how does the pace *feel:* easy, hard, impossible to maintain? Training at 60 percent of your MHRR should seem easy and comfortable. You should be able to carry on a conversation. Conversely, an 85 percent effort should exhaust you within 30 minutes.

Although some exercise physiologists contend that heart rate training is unnecessary for those embarking upon a long-term, high-mileage conditioning program, it is useful for those wishing to derive the most benefit from the least amount of exercise time. In addition, it is a valuable tool for keeping motivated cyclists from exercising too hard. Too many cyclists erroneously believe that if riding hard is good, riding harder is even better. Heart rate training provides a justification to ease the strain.

Incorporate this information in your weekly program by exercising at or above your 60 percent training heart rate. Maintain it for the duration of your long weekend ride and on the days you duplicate your touring pace. Go well above it (75 percent or more) on high-intensity days. Organizing your workouts in this manner will assure continued improvement in aerobic capacity.

Strength to Endure

While aerobic fitness is important for touring cyclists, it's only part of the package. You'll also need enough muscle strength to crank that loaded bike up a long mountain road and keep it under control on the winding descent. The best way to become a stronger, more skilled cyclist is, as cycling legend Eddy Merckx says, to "ride lots."

And, if your goal is touring fitness, you shouldn't be riding just any bike. Different muscles come into play when riding a loaded bicycle as opposed to a 22-pound racer. For instance, it takes more upper-body strength to control a loaded bike when cornering, especially if much of the weight is over the rear wheel. As a result, plan to start riding your touring bike with full panniers weeks before leaving.

While there's no substitute for the task-specific, isometric conditioning of pulling on the handlebar, push-ups and sit-ups will help strengthen the upper body and back muscles so important to loaded touring. Riding a mountain bike off-road will also build your shoulders, arms, and hands. Plus, it's a lot more fun than kissing the carpet 50 times a night.

Pack the panniers for your long weekend rides to familiarize yourself with the idiosyncrasies of handling a loaded bike. One area that demands particular attention is descending. Because of the extra weight, use only top-notch brakes and apply them harder and sooner when entering corners or stopping. As on any bike, brakes should be used intermittently to prevent glazing the pads and overheating the rims.

While you're mastering handling, also fine-tune your riding position and gearing. A handlebar stem that's the perfect height and extension for fast, 25-mile training rides might promote discomfort during a long day in the saddle. Gearing, meanwhile, should be the result of much prudence. Determine the lowest gear ratio you will need and then add a couple of teeth to the largest rear cog, or subtract a couple from the small chainring up front. The lowest ratio should be your bail-out gear, to be used only in near-vertical emergencies. Even twiddling along in a 20-inch gear beats pushing a loaded bike uphill.

A 50-pound load won't allow you the luxury of standing and working the bike from side to side, so get used to climbing while seated and spinning your granny gear. A 1-to-1 gear ratio (i.e., 28-tooth chainring and 28-tooth rear cog) is the minimum if your route has hills. Lower gearing—a larger rear cog and/or smaller inner chainring—is wise for mountainous routes.

Training and practice will ensure that your tour doesn't come to an untimely end because of unexpected aches or unwilling legs, but inadequate mental preparation has probably ended more tours than all physical difficulties combined. We're not just talking about the know-how to fix mechanical problems, although if you can't repair a flat, replace a broken spoke or cable, or true a wheel, you'd better learn. We're talking about cultivating a state of mind that's prepared for dreary weather, headwinds, balky cook stoves, unfriendly natives, and fitful nights in damp, musty sleeping bags.

What's more, even the best of friends, when brought together under the rigors of a long, hard tour, will often come to resent their comrades' annoying habits. Oscar and Felix might enjoy each other's company on a Sunday club ride but not a cross-state tour.

Despite the lure of the open road, extended touring isn't for every cyclist. If you love to ride hard and fast in anticipation of a gourmet meal and a soft bed, you should reconsider taking a two-week tour with friends who like to stop for pictures at every vista and eat rehydrated chili. Before sacrificing any of your precious vacation, test the waters with short weekend rides together. Warning signs include breaking into uncontrollable sobbing over a third flat tire, a tendency to rechart the course around every looming hill, and pitching your bike off a cliff because the forecast calls for rain—again. If this sounds like you, either go it alone or stick to one-day rides.

18 PREPARING FOR A CENTURY

Linda Apriletti of Coral Gables, Florida, would like to forget her first century. Her bike weighed almost 30 pounds. She got lost. She ran out of food. "I just felt miserable," she recalls.

A few months later, she completed her second 100-miler. Her new 21-pound bike worked well. She paced herself. She had plenty to eat and drink. "It was a completely different experience," she says.

Like many other novice century riders, Apriletti learned the hard way how to prepare for a 100-mile event—the sport's most popular type of recreational ride. But your first century needn't be a lesson in pain and frustration. By following a few simple guidelines, you can avoid common mistakes and have an enjoyable ride.

The basis of successful century riding is training. The accompanying ten-week conditioning program is designed for cyclists attempting their first century. It's geared specifically for those who've been riding an average of 45 to 50 miles a week. If you've been riding a bit more, increase the distances slightly.

In table 3-1, "easy" means taking a leisurely ride, "pace" means matching the speed you plan to maintain for the century, and "brisk" means cycling faster than your century pace. If your century ride is on Saturday, move back the final week's training one day (i.e., take Wednesday off and ride 10 miles on Thursday and 5 on Friday).

As you can see, you'll need to find time to train during the week. Try commuting to work, riding at lunch, or using an indoor resistance trainer. Though it's possible to prepare for a century by riding just four days a week, a six-day schedule works best. Remember that easy riding facilitates recovery better than inactivity.

With this schedule, Saturday is crucial. Doing progressively longer distances each weekend is the key to a successful century. It's wise to schedule your long ride for this day so Sunday will be available in case of bad weather or other interruptions.

The goal is to increase mileage by 10 to 12 percent each week. If you simply want to complete the 100 miles, your longest training ride needn't exceed 65 miles. Resist the temptation to drastically boost your weekly mileage, especially as the ride approaches. Overdoing it can lead to staleness, fatigue, and injury. Watch for such overtraining warning signs as restless sleep, fluctuations in morning pulse rate, a sudden drop in weight, and fatigue or listlessness during workouts.

TABLE 3-1.
Goal: To Ride 100 Miles

Week	Mon.	Tues.	Wed.	Thurs.	Fri.	Sat.	Sun.	Total Weekly Mileage
	Easy	Pace	Brisk		Pace	Pace	Pace	
1	6	10	12	Off	10	30	9	77
2	7	11	13	Off	11	34	10	86
3	8	13	15	Off	13	38	11	98
4	8	14	17	Off	14	42	13	108
5	9	15	19	Off	15	47	14	119
6	11	15	21	Off	15	53	16	131
7	12	15	24	Off	15	59	18	143
8	13	15	25	Off	15	65	20	153
9	15	15	25	Off	15	65	20	155
10	15	15	25	Off	10	5 Easy	100	170

But there's more to successful century riding than adhering to training schedules. Here are 15 do's and don'ts—with comments from several century veterans from across the country—that will help make your first century a rewarding experience.

1. Don't wait until you're thirsty to drink. On a warm day, drink two bottles of liquid per hour. John Cook of Roseburg, Oregon, says he drinks half a bottle every 10 miles. "I think water is the key to [a good ride]," he says.

2. Do drink before, during, and after rides to avoid dehydration-induced fatigue. Harry Meyers of Diamond Springs, California, drank more than 3 gallons of liquid when he rode the Davis Double Century, but he still got dehydrated. He says chicken soup helped him finish in about 17 hours.

3. Do consider using an energy drink. These specially designed mixtures will quench your thirst and supply vital glucose. In her second century, Apriletti used a carbohydrate-replacement drink. "It kept me from bonking," she says.

4. Do eat lots of carbohydrates, such as pasta and rice, during the three days prior to the ride. Try fruit, oatmeal, whole-grain cereal, and bread for breakfast the day of the ride.

5. Don't wait until you're hungry to eat during a ride. Recommended snacks include bananas, cookies, and dried fruit. When Jeff Hawkins of Brooklyn, New York, did a 50-mile ride last year, "I didn't bring anything to eat, which was foolish. The last 10 miles, I was hurting pretty bad."

6. Don't stuff yourself. Eat lightly and steadily, filling your pockets with food at rest stops. "I eat every 20 miles," says Cook.

7. Do vary your riding position. Frequently move your hands from the top of the handlebar to the brake lever hoods to the drops. It'll prevent muscle fatigue.

8. Do stretch while you ride. Every 30 minutes stand on the pedals, arch your back, and stretch your legs. To prevent upper-body stiffness, do slow neck rolls and shoulder shrugs.

9. Do divide the ride into segments and prepare a strategy for each. "Try to stay away from people who are trying to 'win' the century ride," says Apriletti.

10. Don't dwell on the miles remaining if you're getting tired. Instead, concentrate on form, efficiency, and drinking and eating adequately. "Give yourself plenty of time and try not to hurry," says Cook. "Just plan on finishing and enjoying it."

11. Don't stop for more than 10 minutes. Longer rest breaks can make you stiff and sap your motivation.

12. Do make sure your bike is properly geared for the course. Ask the ride organizer or someone who has ridden the route previously for recommendations.

13. Do wear cycling shoes that fit comfortably, cycling shorts with chamois, and padded cycling gloves. Sunglasses protect your eyes and reduce fatigue from glare. "Bicycle shorts make a world of difference," says Hawkins.

14. Do cycle with someone who has similar goals. "Ride with other people so you get support and encouragement," says Apriletti.

15. Do believe in yourself. Completing your first century is within your grasp. Think positive.

▮19▮ BECOMING A RACER

During a talk on training at the 1987 Hotter 'n Hell Hundred in Wichita Falls, Texas, a tentative hand went up in the audience. "I'd like to start racing," said an apprehensive young man, "but I'm not sure I'm ready. I can keep up in group rides, I like centuries, and I can even drop some local racers on hills. But I'm nervous about competing. Should I just forget it?"

Good question. There's no reason to race if you don't want to. Cycling should be a pleasurable activity. If racing isn't fun, ignore peer pressure and don't do it. Just say no.

But there are many reasons for competing, even if you're apprehensive about speeding through corners in a thicket of handlebars or putting your ego on the line in a time trial. For starters, racing is exciting. The speed, the adrenaline, and the action make competition a peak experience, an emotional step up from everyday riding. Racing is a social activity as well. You'll meet fitness-oriented people at events and in your local club. Plus, racing is a great motivator because it encourages you to structure your training around upcoming events.

But you don't have to compete to reap the benefits of a racer's training program. The speed you develop from training like a racer will enable you to keep up with synchronized traffic lights and rocket out of danger in tight urban situations. The endurance you build will let you have more fun on tours and group rides. And by learning to plan your training so you peak for important events, you'll be fresher, faster, and fitter at the end of the season. Simply put, race training will help you become a better bike rider.

This chapter will teach you the basics of race training. You'll get advice from experienced racers, as well as two of the nation's best cycling coaches—Walter Golebiewski and Len Pettyjohn. All you need to start is some basic riding experience, a reasonable level of fitness, and a desire to race or at least apply the elements of a racer's training program to your recreational cycling.

Be Patient

Becoming a competent racer takes time. Cycling requires complex skills such as endurance, quick reflexes, and anaerobic power that may take several years to develop. It's mentally demanding, too, because race strategy requires instantaneous decisions.

"The development process takes a minimum of five years," says Golebiewski. "It doesn't matter what level of competition you're at—from juniors to masters. After five years you should be able to answer the question, 'Am I in the right sport?' "

There are exceptions, of course. Mark Waite, a member of the 1988 U.S. Olympic long team, progressed more quickly. "If you have an athletic background," says Waite, a former runner, "and the athletic mentality is there, it can take less time—maybe three or four years."

As a result, don't get discouraged if you aren't on the victory podium after your first race. "Often, novices get upset that they aren't doing great," says Golebiewski. "They don't understand this is normal."

Set Appropriate Goals

Your goals in cycling depend on your age, the time you can devote to the sport, your body type, and the availability of good competition. If you're 33 years old, don't aim for the Tour de France. A top placing in masters competition (30 and older) is a more realistic goal. But if you're 14, a pro career may be a viable goal. Likewise, if you can only spare an hour of daily training amid career and family responsibilities, don't set your heart on the Race Across America. But an hour a day is still plenty to excel in the short criteriums and time trials typical of entry-level racing. Goals don't have to be related to competition, either. "You can have short-term goals with your friends in training," says Pettyjohn. "Shoot for a 10-second pull in a paceline this week and then increase it to 15 the next."

You must also realistically assess your body type. If you're muscular and stocky, emphasize flat and fast events. Conversely, if you're lean and willowy, look for hilly races. "New racers should learn what their physiological handicaps are," says Kent Bostick, 1987 national road champion. "Then they can train to be successful within these limitations." As Pettyjohn explains, a race that's important to a lean climber isn't going to be important to a strong, 6-foot-4, 205-pound time trialist.

Finally, achievable goals depend largely on the amount of racing available in your area. "Racing is the best training," says Waite, so if you can't compete often, you won't progress as rapidly as those who can. Plus, if you have to drive 300 miles every weekend to find a 20-mile criterium, you'll quickly lose your enthusiasm.

If you can race frequently, Pettyjohn suggests setting a sequence of goals. "Your first goal should be to finish with the field," he says. "Next, get to the front at least once during the race. Then, think of a certain placing—maybe the top 20. If you're successful, try to win a prime. Finally, shoot for a win."

Join a Cycling Club

When you join a club, you immediately inherit a group of experienced training partners. "The whole philosophy of racing," explains Golebiewski, "is economy of effort—how to save energy for the last part of the race. Group rides create a racing environment in which you'll learn bike handling and how to draft a wheel."

A club also supplies invaluable motivation. When you've scheduled a ride with friends, for instance, it's that much tougher to cancel. Club rides help novices gauge their race readiness, too. When you can keep up with experienced competitors in training, you're probably ready to try your first race.

Often, a sponsored club will even lend financial support to some of its most promising riders, a vital benefit in a sport where equipment and travel can become expensive.

Get a Coach

"A coach is almost a necessity for a beginning rider," says Waite. Without one, you may never be sure you're training properly.

Many good racing clubs have capable instructors who have attended U.S. Cycling Federation (USCF) coaching clinics. They know the latest techniques in training, nutrition, and race strategy. Even better is a coach experienced enough to be certified by the USCF.

Still, it's often difficult finding a knowledgeable instructor. "The biggest problem with most coaches," says Pettyjohn, "is they coach according to a formula. They don't understand that even two riders of similar abilities are going to have different peaks and valleys of performance."

Experienced racers can be good coaches. In fact, many riders are anxious to pass on the tricks of the trade but are seldom asked. Try approaching one of the top finishers after a race and asking advice.

Don't get discouraged if you can't find a good coach. Instead, Pettyjohn suggests letting your body be your guide. In fact, despite your relative inexperience, you may be your own best coach. Read all you can about the sport, observe good riders, ask questions after races, and keep careful records of your training. In time, you'll come to know what works and what doesn't. Even if you start with a coach, Waite says you may want to "go on your own once you get a feel for it."

Fine-Tune Your Position

Bike fit is one area where a good coach or an experienced riding partner can provide immediate help. Indeed, you can follow the most precise mathematical formulas and still look like a frog on the bike. An astute rider, though, will be able to suggest small adjustments that will make big differences after watching you pedal for just 10 minutes. If you don't know any experienced cyclists, Pettyjohn advises looking at yourself in a mirror or on videotape.

Ride in Bad Weather

Racers consider early-season training vital, but unfortunately, early-season weather in most of the country is bad. It snows in Michigan, rains in Oregon, and the spring winds blow everywhere. But if you head for the couch the minute it clouds up, you'll never log enough miles to be competitive.

"Most of the time I'll go out in any weather to train," says Waite, who lives in Colorado Springs (elevation, 6,000 feet). "Sometimes I ride in the snow for fun."

By training in nasty weather, you'll build the necessary confidence to handle inclement race conditions. For instance, 7-Eleven's Andy Hampsten, who won the 1988 Tour of Italy with an epic ride through snow and sleet, attributed his mental toughness to training in similar conditions in Boulder, Colorado. In addition, riding in the spring slop will hone your bike-handling skills.

Build a Mileage Base

March and April is the time to build a mileage base. Once or twice a week, go for long rides. (The duration should be equal to the time it will take to complete your longest race.) Ride in a gear you can spin at 90 to 100 rpm at a heart rate of 70 to 80 percent of your maximum (220 minus your age for men, 226 for women). Use a heart rate monitor or the "talk test"—if you're too out of breath to carry on a conversation, you're riding too fast.

As for mileage goals, most coaches recommend logging at least 500 miles at an aerobic pace before beginning hard training or racing. Don't try to duplicate the sometimes astronomical mileage weeks of the pros, though. "Remember, you can't do the training that more experienced riders can," cautions Golebiewski. "Quality is more important."

Build a Power Base

Entry-level racers usually have the endurance for their typically short events but lack the power to stay with the pack during climbs and sprints. Once you have a mileage base, how can you develop a suitable motor? During the early season, Pettyjohn suggests riding a mountain bike off-road, especially when it's cold. "You can ride a mountain bike when it's 10 degrees and get an incredibly good power workout," he explains, citing the greater rolling resistance and slower speed. "If you tried to go out on your road bike, you would freeze."

As the weather improves, Waite advocates a lot of on-road climbing. Maintain a steady cadence on long hills and sprint up short ones. Pettyjohn also suggests a weekly 10-mile time trial and keeping a log of your times to chart improvement.

Finally, do some two-, three-, or four-person team time trials. According to Pettyjohn, "In an individual time trial you use a big gear and lose leg speed. But with other riders it becomes a faster and much harder event."

Develop Bike-Handling Skills

No matter how much power you have, you must stay upright to win. "The biggest problem in cycling isn't physiology," says Pettyjohn. "It's mastering the experience of riding fast with a group and changing direction. There's a lot of strong riders who don't have a problem staying with the field—until they come to a corner. Then they're all over each other."

To hone your bike-handling skills, try jamming on a mountain bike through mud, snow, or dicey terrain. "It's fun and it builds confidence," says Pettyjohn. "You can hang the bike out in ways you never could on the road."

Another way to prepare for pack riding is by doing group bike-handling drills. Although Pettyjohn says nothing can prepare you for "the adrenaline rush, the sheer terror of getting in among other racers," he suggests a modified king of the mountain game that involves riding old bikes on a soft surface. "Ride at each other from the side, from behind, and do a lot of bumping. The only rule is you can't take your hands off the bar. You'll get used to riding close and learn to handle bumps and pushes without panicking and falling." To protect yourself, wear a long-sleeved jersey, old tights, a good helmet, and maybe even elbow pads. Don't go too fast, though—5 or 6 mph is plenty.

Likewise, ride with others on the road. Find two or three training partners and get used to riding within inches of each other as you maintain a fast paceline.

Finally, since even the best bike handlers take an occasional spill, do some tumbling drills—forward rolls, shoulder rolls—the whole gym class routine.

"Most riders don't know how to fall off the bike," says Golebiewski. "Tumbling is your preparation for future crashes."

The Equipment You'll Need

Most novice riders worry too much about equipment. The striking technical advances in frames and componentry during the past five years—nonferrous tubesets, index shifting, step-in pedals, tighter geometries—mean that even moderately priced bikes are better than those raced by pros a few years ago. What's more, since these advances have been spurred by a highly competitive market, medium-priced bikes from different manufacturers are usually of equally good value. This means you no longer have to spend big bucks for race-worthy equipment.

Your best source of advice for racing equipment is a professional bike shop. Chris Caunt, owner of the Criterium Bike Shop in Colorado Springs, Colorado, outfits numerous novice racers who are inspired by top riders at the nearby Olympic Training Center. For those with a background in touring or fitness riding, he recommends a moderately priced, steep-angled racing frame with either Shimano 105 or equivalent SunTour components.

"Beginners shouldn't invest in an expensive racing frame because they're probably going to crash," he says. "And young racers may grow out of their first frame in a year or two."

Such a moderately priced bike usually comes with clincher wheels. Caunt says these are fine for lower-category racing, but as you improve, he recommends upgrading to a set of high-quality tubular wheels.

"But there's a big overlap between clincher tire performance and that of tubulars," explains Caunt. "Clincher rims weigh about 100 grams more than the lightest and most expensive tubular rims, but they weigh about the same as medium-priced tubulars." Thus, there's little point in trading in good clincher equipment for comparatively priced tubulars. In fact, Italian Roberto Gaggioli won the 1988 U.S. CoreStates Pro Championship on clinchers.

Make sure your bike is geared for racing. If your free-wheel is a wide-ratio model more suited for touring, replace it with a tighter cluster. But don't let your ego displace common sense. If you race on hilly courses, that stock 13-23T will save your knees. On steep climbs, you may even spin by the straight-block riders struggling in 42×19.

Don't spend all of your racing budget on the bike. "We're frustrated when would-be racers buy the most expensive bike they can afford but can't buy the accessories they need," says Caunt. He recommends purchasing cleated shoes, a patch kit, a frame pump, two water bottles and cages, several pairs of riding shorts, basic tools, an ANSI- or Snell-certified helmet (a requirement in USCF races), and a car rack for transporting your bike.

If you can't afford a new racing bicycle, you can probably outfit your current bike for entry-level events by upgrading the wheels, amending the gearing, and making other basic refinements. Again, your local bike shop can help you with the particulars.

Racing Divisions

The USCF classifies racers according to age, sex, and ability. Age groups include a junior division for riders under 17; an open or senior division for 18- to 29-year-olds; and a masters (formerly veteran) division for those over 30. The latter is subdivided into five-year age brackets. Men and women compete in separate classifications.

The senior division is organized according to ability, from Category IV (novice) to Category I. Riders must place three times in the top three, or six times in the top six, and obtain a bike-handling recommendation in order to advance to a higher category.

To get a USCF license, ask your local bike shop for an application. Or write the U.S. Cycling Federation, 1750 E. Boulder St., Colorado Springs, CO 80909. The annual cost is $32.

Training Schedule: February to May 15 (for a first race in May)

February

Goals:
1. Build overall body strength.
2. Develop general aerobic fitness.
3. Improve body control and coordination.

Sample Week:

Monday: Weight training and tumbling drills
Tuesday: Aerobic workout: ride road bike, mountain bike or indoor trainer, run, cross-country ski, swim, etc.
Wednesday: Same as Monday
Thursday: Same as Tuesday
Friday: Same as Monday
Saturday: Rest
Sunday: Long aerobic workout: group ride, run, ski, hike, swim, etc.

March

Goals:
1. Develop upper-body strength.
2. Begin developing specific aerobic power on the bike.
3. Improve bike-handling and pack-riding skills.

Sample Week:

Monday: 20-minute warm-up on indoor trainer, weight training
Tuesday: Off-road ride
Wednesday: Aerobic workout: steady cycling on the road if possible; indoor riding or an aerobic equivalent such as running if not
Thursday: Same as Monday

Friday: Aerobic-paced road ride followed by bike-handling drills
Saturday: Rest
Sunday: Long group ride

April to May 15

Goals:
1. Maintain upper-body strength.
2. Continue building power on the bike.
3. Work on bike handling in group rides and club races.

Sample Week:
Monday: Rest
Tuesday: Medium-length ride with hills, or criterium practice with your club
Wednesday: Steady, medium-length ride followed by light upper-body weight exercises such as push-ups, pull-ups, sit-ups, and neck bridges
Thursday: Medium-length ride with intervals, or a fast group ride with cyclists a bit stronger than you
Friday: Short, easy ride and light exercises for the upper body
Saturday: Rest, or short easy spin
Sunday: Long, hard group ride, or training race

If this program doesn't fit your work schedule, adjust it accordingly. For instance, take one weekday off instead of Saturday. Be sure to maintain the suggested workout sequence, however.

Training Camps

Each year the USCF sponsors inexpensive, four-day development clinics at its three Olympic Training Centers (Colorado Springs, Colorado; Lake Placid, New York; and Marquette, Michigan). These are open to all riders, including juniors, women, and masters. They're conducted by national team coaches and riders. The only prerequisite for attending is that you're a USCF license holder.

Typically, each day begins with light calisthenics followed by breakfast. At 9:00 A.M. there's a meeting to discuss the day's agenda, and at 10:00, a training ride. During these rides, the coaches and national team members work with small groups, emphasizing technique and positioning. Afterward, there's time for a shower and lunch. At 2:00 P.M. there's a lecture or demonstration on such topics as bike fit, planning a yearly training schedule, race strategy, weight training, physiology, nutrition, and so on. Then it's time for dinner and another lecture or a cycling movie. The evening session ends at about 9:00 P.M., and lights out is at 10:00.

These clinics are held at various times during the year. The fee covers everything except transportation to and from the camp. For more information or to apply, write USCF Development Clinics at the address given previously, or call (719) 578-4581.

There are also development programs for budding track racers at many U.S. velodromes. Here is a list of American tracks with some type of instructional classes. Write the one nearest you for more information.

Alkek Velodrome (Houston, Texas)
Houston Park and Recreation Dept.
2999 S. Wayside
Houston, TX 77023

Alpenrose Velodrome (Portland, Oregon)
Mike Murray
1632 Birdsdale
Gresham, OR 97030

Baton Rouge Velodrome (Baton Rouge, Louisiana)
3140 N. Sherwood Forest Blvd.
Baton Rouge, LA 70809

Brown Deer Velodrome (Milwaukee, Wisconsin)
Milwaukee Wheelmen
2607 N. Downer
Milwaukee, WI 53211

Dick Lane Velodrome (East Point, Georgia)
1431 Norman Berry Dr.
East Point, GA 30344

Dorais Velodrome (Detroit, Michigan)
Wolverine Sports Club
Box 63
Royal Oak, MI 48068

Encino Velodrome (Encino, California)
Southern California Cycling Federation
Box 713
Torrance, CA 90508-0713

Kissena Velodrome (Flushing, New York)
New York Bicycling Federation
87-66 256th St.
Floral Park, NY 11001

Lehigh County Velodrome (Trexlertown,
    Pennsylvania)
217 Main St.
Emmaus, PA 18049

Major Taylor Velodrome (Indianapolis, Indiana)
Chuck Quast
3649 Cold Spring Rd.
Indianapolis, IN 46222

Marymoor Velodrome (Redmond, Washington)
Washington State Bicycling Assoc.
Box 15633
Seattle, WA 98115

Meadowhill Park Velodrome (Northbrook, Illinois)
Northbrook Cycling Committee
422 S. Gibbons
Arlington Heights, IL 60004

St. Louis Velodrome (St. Louis, Missouri)
Box 15102
St. Louis, MO 63110

San Diego Velodrome (San Diego, California)
2221 Morley Field Dr.
San Diego, CA 92104

Santa Clara County Velodrome (San Jose, California)
Northern California Cycling Assoc.
845 Juanita Dr.
Walnut Creek, CA 94595

7-Eleven Olympic Velodrome (Carson, California)
1000 E. Victoria
Carson, CA 90747

7-Eleven Velodrome (Colorado Springs, Colorado)
U.S. Olympic Committee
1776 E. Boulder
Colorado Springs, CO 80909

Washington Bowl (Kenosha, Wisconsin)
Box 863
Kenosha, WI 53141

20 WHAT AILS YOU?

As with most athletes, cyclists can experience a variety of discomforts. This handy guide will help you pinpoint your problem and then use the proper remedy.

Hands

Ailment
Numbness and loss of grip strength (ulnar neuropathy).
Cause
Excessive hand pressure on the handlebar.
Solutions
Wear cycling gloves with padded palms or pad the handlebar; change hand position frequently while riding.

Lower Back

Ailments
Stiffness; soreness.

Causes
1. Leaning over the handlebar for extended periods of time.
2. Handlebar too low in relation to saddle.
3. Long handlebar stem extension.
4. Leg length discrepancy.

Solutions
1. Stretch before every ride, vary your riding position, and do bent-knee sit-ups to strengthen the muscles that support the spine.
2. Raise the handlebar.
3. Substitute a handlebar stem with the proper extension. (When riding with hands on the brake lever hoods, the front hub should be obscured by the handlebar.)
4. Put a shim between the cleat and shoe on the shorter leg, or have a podiatrist design an orthotic or shoe insert.

Eyes

Ailments
Fatigue; dryness.

Causes
1. Overexposure to ultraviolet (UV) radiation.
2. Wind penetration and/or poor tearing.

Solutions
1. Wear sunglasses with shatterproof lenses designed to block a high percentage of UV radiation.
2. Wear wraparound-style sunglasses and/or use a wetting solution.

Feet

Ailment
Burning or numbness in ball of foot ("hot foot").

Causes
1. Narrow shoes.
2. Stiff plastic soles.
3. Tight toe straps.
Solutions
1. Wear cycling shoes that fit snugly but are not too tight.
2. Install a thin cushion insole.
3. Loosen toe straps or switch to a clipless pedal system.

Shoulders

Ailments
Stiffness; soreness.
Causes
1. Riding with locked elbows.
2. Improper handlebar width.
3. Improper handlebar stem extension and/or height.
Solutions
1. Keep elbows bent to absorb road shock.
2. Substitute a properly sized handlebar. (Generally, handlebar width should match your shoulder width.)
3. Substitute a handlebar stem with the proper extension and height. (When riding with hands on the brake lever hoods, the front hub should be obscured by the handlebar.)

Neck

Ailments
Stiffness; pain.
Causes
1. Heavy helmet.
2. Stationary head position.
3. Riding position too far forward.
Solutions
1. Wear a lighter helmet that meets accepted safety standards.
2. Periodically tilt your head from side to side while riding.

3. Raise the handlebar for a more upright riding position or substitute a shorter stem extension.

Thighs

Ailments
Soreness; cramps.
Causes
1. Exceptionally hard or prolonged effort.
2. Improper training and/or fluid replacement.
Solutions
1. Massage the area and rest.
2. Gradually increase mileage and intensity during the season, and drink frequently while riding.

Buttocks

Ailments
Discomfort; chafing; saddle sores.
Causes
1. Lack of training and/or saddle that's too narrow, wide, or hard.
2. Inadequate riding apparel.
3. Lack of cleanliness.
Solutions
1. Gradually increase mileage and/or substitute a properly sized saddle. (Women, for instance, require a wider seat.) A saddle pad might also help.
2. Wear multipanel cycling shorts with a soft chamois.
3. Cleanse the groin area before and after every ride; wash shorts after every ride.

Knees

Ailments
Stiffness; discomfort; pain.
Causes
1. Pushing too big a gear.

2. Increasing mileage too rapidly.
3. Improper cleat position.
4. Incorrect saddle height.
5. Inadequate clothing.
Solutions
1. Learn to spin a small gear at a brisk cadence (90-plus revolutions per minute).
2. Increase mileage and intensity only about 10 percent per week during the season.
3. Position cleats so that the ball of each foot is directly above the pedal axle.
4. Position the saddle so each knee bends slightly at the bottom of each pedal stroke.
5. Wear tights when the temperature dips below 65°F.

Waist

Ailment
Side stitch.
Cause
Inadequate oxygen delivery to muscles used in heavy breathing.
Solution
Reduce intensity of effort and/or lightly massage area to increase blood flow.

Ankles

Ailment
Tenderness at the back of the ankle (Achilles tendinitis).
Causes
1. Improper warm-up.
2. Climbing in too big a gear.
3. Improper saddle height and/or cleat position.
Solutions
1. Stretch beforehand; start rides gradually.
2. Use lower gears for climbing.
3. Adjust saddle height and/or cleat position for proper leg extension and orientation (see Knee solutions).

Hips

Ailments
Chronic soreness; contusion.
Causes
1. Improper saddle height and/or leg length discrepancy.
2. Crashing.
Solutions
   1. Adjust saddle height so there's a slight bend in each leg at the bottom of the pedal stroke; put a shim between cleat and shoe of the shorter leg, or have a podiatrist design an orthotic or shoe insert.
   2. Apply ice periodically until swelling subsides, then resume easy riding; improve bike-handling skills.

Lower Arms and Legs

Ailment
Minor abrasions (road rash).
Cause
Crashing.
Solutions
   Clean wound thoroughly and cover with an antibiotic salve and breathable dressing, which should be changed daily; improve bike-handling skills.

Skin

Ailments
Sunburn; skin cancer.
Cause
Overexposure to ultraviolet (UV) radiation.
Solutions
   1. Use sunscreen with a minimum sun protection factor (SPF) of 15.
   2. Cover burned areas with a visor, tights, or a long-sleeved jersey to prevent further damage; see a doctor about suspicious lesions and moles.

21 75 TIPS FOR SHAPING UP, LOSING WEIGHT, AND RIDING BETTER

Cycling is ostensibly a simple sport, but it's also rife with tricks and tidbits that can help you ride faster, longer, and more comfortably with fewer problems. Indeed, any rider with more than a season in his or her legs can probably find truth in the statement, "If I only knew then what I know now." With this in mind, we pooled our collective knowledge and present our 75 best tips for shaping up, losing weight, and riding better.

1. A cold/cool-weather rule of thumb: If you're comfortable in the first mile, you're dressed too warmly.

2. Wrap tape around your road bike's seatpost where it enters the frame so you can relocate your ideal saddle height if the post slips or is removed. Also, memorize or record the distance from the center of your pedal axle to the top of the saddle—it's handy when traveling or borrowing a bike.

3. Rotate your tires. The rear wears more than twice as fast as the front, so switch them every 1,000 miles to get maximum life.

4. To lose weight, ride at midday. Not only will you burn calories, but the exercise will suppress your appetite. Afterward, lunch can consist of an apple or a cup of low-calorie yogurt.

5. When your chain derails in front, don't immediately dismount. Instead, try gently shifting it back on while pedaling. If this doesn't work, you needn't dirty your hands. Invert the bike so the chain catches on the bottom of the small chainring. Then grasp the pedal and turn it backward to fully engage the chain.

6. On days when motivation is lacking, remove the pressure to do a specific workout. Explore a new route and enjoy the scenery. At the end of the ride you may be surprised to find that your average speed was almost training pace.

7. The most nutritious fast foods are Chinese, Mexican, and Italian. These generally have less fat and are higher in carbohydrates than other cuisines.

8. To smooth a jerky pedal stroke, practice pedaling *down* a long, gradual hill in a low gear (e.g., 42×17) as fast as possible without bouncing in the saddle.

9. When mixing sports drinks, put less-concentrated solution into the bottle(s) you'll drink last. Drinks always taste sweeter the longer you ride, and what seems pleasant initially can taste syrupy 3 hours later.

10. Take a cue from fighters who shadow box to refine technique. Early or late in the day, watch your shadow as you ride, checking for flaws in position, form, and pedaling style.

11. In winter, wear a balaclava under your helmet. Regular hats are bulky and may require changing helmet pads.

12. When climbing, think of yourself as pedaling *across* the stroke, rather than up and down. Strive to apply power from the back to the front. This maintains momentum while utilizing all your leg muscles.

13. To save valuable time in a mountain bike race, drill an extra valve hole in your rim and insert a second, uninflated tube in the tire. If the first tube goes flat, you can simply inflate the second.

14. To reduce your consumption of calorie-rich party food and appetite-stimulating alcohol, start every celebration with a club soda or mineral water. It'll help fill you up so you're less inclined to overindulge.

15. The best way to recover from a hard effort is to ride easily the next day rather than take the day off. Use the opportunity to cycle with family and friends who are normally "too slow."

16. For a fun and unique diversion from cycling, try "skiing" on pavement with in-line skates such as Rollerblades. They're compact, easy on your knees, and most important, strengthen the cycling muscles.

17. When doing quality training such as intervals, use a heart rate monitor. Determine your anaerobic threshold by observing at what heart rate you can time trial

for 5 miles. Then do intervals within a range 10 percent below this rate.

18. Carry a spare tube *and* patch kit, so you're not disabled if you have two flats on a ride. Also, always carry a spare tube in the rain. Flats occur more frequently, and it's difficult to apply patches when it's wet. Check the glue in your patch kit periodically to be sure it hasn't dried.

19. When you have finished your lower-body winter weight-training program, go directly to intervals and climbing workouts on the bike. If you follow weight training with a month or more of slow-paced endurance rides, you'll lose some of the strength and power you gained. Add endurance training later in the spring.

20. Before a race, crumple your paper number and then attach it with extra pins. This keeps it from billowing while you ride.

21. To receive free maps for a tour, as well as excellent brochures on accommodations, attractions, climate, and history, contact the tourism office of the state you'll be visiting and the chambers of commerce in the towns through which you'll be riding.

22. Use nylon-reinforced strapping tape as a protective rim strip. It's light and thin (to aid tire installation and removal) and doesn't migrate to uncover spoke heads. For narrow rims, tear the tape lengthwise.

23. Carry $5 and some change in your tire repair kit. You can buy a snack on long rides, phone home if you have a mechanical problem, or pay a driver to drop you off.

24. If you have less than an hour to train, emphasize quality. Warm up by spinning easily for 10 minutes. Do five 15-second sprints with 45 seconds between them, then ten intervals comprising 1 minute on and 1 minute off. Cool down for 10 minutes.

25. Write your name, address, phone number, and "this bike was stolen" on a piece of masking tape and stick it to the fork's steerer tube. Then if it ever is, a shop mechanic may someday contact you in the midst of a repair and make your day.

26. If you hate headwinds, plan routes that avoid them. Use mountains, tree lines, valleys, and houses to shield you until you turn around and can enjoy a tailwind.

27. To stave off fatigue during hard, sustained pedaling, learn to "float" each leg every three or four strokes. Let your foot fall without pushing. Time trial specialist Jacques Anquetil reportedly used this technique.

28. When full-finger gloves are necessary, unwrap, slice, and repackage your snacks before riding. This makes it easier to grab a bite-size morsel while cycling.

29. For dusk rides, carry two reflective leg bands, a portable light, and a reflective triangle or vest in your jersey pocket so you can get home safely.

30. Develop bike-handling skills by riding with others on a grassy field. Play tag, ride the length of the field leaning into another rider, or pick up sticks without dismounting. Falling on soft ground won't hurt at slow speed.

31. Check your tires after every ride for embedded pieces of glass or stone and remove them to prevent a future flat.

32. To satisfy a cookie craving, eat fig bars or graham crackers, which are relatively low in fat.

33. If you ruin a 700C clincher tire but a riding partner has a spare sew-up, use it to get home. (Go slowly and avoid sharp corners and bumps.)

34. When mountain biking over terrain that requires frequent portages, carry as much weight as possible on your person. Use a fanny pack if necessary.

35. Leave some slack in the front derailleur cable. This way, the lever needn't be flush with the down tube when using the small chainring, making it easier to grasp.

36. The next time you're struggling on a tough climb, smile. You'll be surprised at its beneficial effect. Also, think "light." Imagine that you weigh half of what you do—that you're a feather on the pedals.

37. Pay careful attention to brake pad condition on mountain bikes. Pads wear quickly and can hit the tire or go into the spokes.

38. Don't grasp the handlebar drops when climbing because it compresses the diaphragm and inhibits breathing. Instead, use the bar top.

39. Check tire inflation at least weekly on road bikes and monthly on mountain bikes. Underinflated tires are slow, wear quickly, and can cause flats or rim damage.

40. For motivation, keep a training diary and use a cyclecomputer. Log your daily mileage (and other data), and tally the miles each week.

41. When touring, carry emergency spokes made by cutting the heads off extra-long spokes and putting two 90-degree bends at the end. These can be installed without removing the freewheel.

42. Helmets shouldn't be tipped back, causing them to catch wind and expose the forehead. Adjust the four retention straps to have equal tension when the helmet is level.

43. Every six months squeeze brake levers and inspect the cables inside for fraying. Replace if necessary.

44. On long rides, do a couple of 15-second sprints every 45 minutes or so. You'll relieve saddle pressure, add variety, and develop speed.

45. Most rear index derailleur problems can be cured by turning the cable's barrel adjuster counterclockwise half a turn. Similarly, if you develop a problem with your index shifting system during a ride and it has a friction backup, switch to that mode to get home.

46. Always put your left foot down when stopping to prevent chainring "tattoos" on your right leg.

47. Align tire labels with valve stems during installation. Then, after finding a hole in the tube, you can locate the corresponding spot on the tire and check for embedded material.

48. Test sports drinks or energy foods long before an important event, since some might upset your stomach.

49. Use rubbing alcohol to install stubborn mountain bike grips. It supplies lubrication but quickly evaporates, leaving them secure.

50. If climbing isn't your forte, start hills at the front of the group and gradually drift back. This way, you'll still be with everyone at the top.

51. Silence annoying clicks and creaks in clipless pedals by applying a few drops of oil to the cleat where it contacts the pedal and to the pedal-gripping hardware.

52. On a narrow road with no shoulder, take the lane to prevent cars from passing when it's not safe, then move over when opposing traffic clears.

53. Install a mountain bike pump behind the seat tube if possible. This frees the main triangle for accessories and eases carrying.

54. If you have squeaky brakes and the pads are properly toed-in, try sanding the rims thoroughly with medium emery cloth. This removes the anodization that sometimes causes pads to grab.

55. Avoid painted roadway markings and metal grates when it's wet. These are especially slippery when it starts raining, before road grime and oil can be washed away.

56. Wrap a spare tubular in cloth or stow it in a saddle bag to prevent sidewall damage.

57. Communication is key to safe group rides. Make sure everyone knows of approaching turns, stops, and hazards.

58. In bad spring weather, ride a mountain bike on the road. You'll save your road bike from rust and build power pushing the heavier bike and fat tires.

59. Keep handlebar ends plugged so they won't take a core sample of your thigh in a crash.

60. Freeze a bottle of water for hot rides. It'll slowly melt, supplying you with cool, refreshing liquid. Conversely, fill your bottle with hot water for cold rides.

61. Put a knobbier, wider tire on the front wheel of your mountain bike to keep from sliding out in corners.

62. If you don't have a chance to slow for an obstacle such as railroad tracks or a pothole, lift your front wheel over them. You may still damage your rear wheel, but at least you won't crash.

63. When servicing your headset, place a section of

inner tube around the lower race during reassembly to keep out dirt and water.

64. In order to commute unencumbered and have clean, pressed clothes at work, drive once a week, using the opportunity to bring in 4 day's worth of attire.

65. In a pinch, a toe-strap buckle can work as a screwdriver.

66. During the season, take 10 minutes twice a week after riding to do strength maintenance exercises such as pull-ups, push-ups, crunches for the abdominals, and neck bridges.

67. Grease the quick-release and mounting bolt threads on your automobile rack to prevent freezing or breakage due to rust.

68. Fit riding into family car trips by cycling one way.

69. When touring, carry a rivet extractor for installing or removing the chain. It's almost impossible to improvise when you don't have one, and it's small, light, and inexpensive.

70. Wear a T-shirt under your jersey when racing. The two will slide against each other in a crash, limiting road rash.

71. To (briefly) foil a thief, adjust one brake so that when its quick-release is closed, it clamps the rim and prevents forward motion, or temporarily undo the front wheel's quick-release. Also, remove or secure your mountain bike's quick-release seat and seatpost when leaving your bike unattended.

72. To loosen a stiff chain link, bend it laterally with your hands.

73. If you plan to start racing this season, do some club time trials and criteriums before entering U.S. Cycling Federation events. The time trials will help you gauge your speed, while the criteriums will furnish important bike-handling and tactical lessons.

74. A cotton cycling cap, carried in your jersey pocket, can provide a lot of warmth when you need it. Much body heat is lost through the head.

75. Shift with the upcoming terrain in mind. Stay on the large chainring if a descent is approaching, or shift to the small ring before a hill. Always be in the appropriate gear prior to a steep ascent.

Part Four
FIRST-CLASS INFO

![22] QUESTIONS AND ANSWERS

Here are some common training and fitness questions asked by new riders like yourself. The answers are provided by *Bicycling* magazine's Fitness Advisory Board, a panel of experts in the cycling/health field.

Speed or Distance?

I'm a new rider who cycles to firm my legs, lose weight, and stay healthy. I ride 15 to 20 miles, four or five days a week. To reach my goals, should I be riding for speed or distance? And should I be cycling every day? Sherri Sharpe, Leesburg, Ga.

Firming muscles, losing weight, and staying healthy are three major reasons people exercise. To realize such goals, you need to ride for speed *and* endurance. Your training week should contain these three components:

Moderate days. To lose weight, forget about the clock and ride moderate distances at a comfortable pace. For you, this will entail two or three 15-mile rides per week. Such a workout will burn fat, as opposed to the carbohydrates that fuel short, intense efforts.

Endurance days. To improve your stamina, go on one long ride every week. For you, this might be 40 to 60 miles. Don't worry about time. Your goal should be to complete the distance.

Speed days. These are crucial to cardiovascular improvement and muscle tone. Twice a week, try to complete 15 miles in an hour while maintaining a cadence of 85 to 90 rpm. Gradually increase speed and distance as you become fitter.

This schedule, which allows for at least one day of rest a week, will bring you all the benefits cycling has to offer. *Christine L. Wells, Ph.D.*

Climbing Technique

I usually climb in a low gear while seated. I have no trouble keeping up with riders who are out of the saddle in a higher gear. I'm planning a mountainous, one-day ride and have been told that I should learn to ride out of the saddle for long distances. Is this true? What's the best climbing technique? Stephanie Jay, Seattle, Wash.

In general, the seated position with hands atop the handlebar is more common and efficient and is typically used for long, steady climbing. The standing position, while less efficient, can deliver more power or torque to the pedals and is often used to accelerate through a short change in grade. Riders also stand to change body position and relieve stress.

Many cyclists believe that standing is better because your entire body weight is used to pedal. If, however, your weight is being used to push the pedal, then an effort also must be made to pull it back to the original position. This ultimately requires more energy than seated riding, but may feel better because the total work, while greater, is shared by muscles of the arms and back.

I recommend experimenting with different climbing positions and practicing making a smooth transition between them. Some riders prefer to shift to a higher gear when they stand. This is appropriate only if you're using a freewheel with closely spaced gears. Whatever you do, don't lock yourself into a climbing position that isn't comfortable just because someone tells you it's better. Use the position that works best for you. *Steve Johnson, Ph.D.*

Becoming a Better Climber

Is there any off-bike training I can do to become a better climber? What about lifting weights and running stairs?
Jeff Singer, Maple Grove, Minn.

Traditional weight lifting doesn't develop aerobic power or efficiency. Any increase in strength you might realize by following such a program will be offset by the added bulk you'll have to pull uphill. Running stairs, while aerobically beneficial, jars your knees. For the kind of leg strength and lung power you need, stay on the bike and take on the mountains. If you don't have any nearby, you can hone your climbing skills with certain flatland techniques. For instance, some people like to stand up and attack a hill in a relatively high gear, while others prefer to shift to a low gear and spin. Good hill training incorporates both these styles. On the flats, alternately practice spinning at 90 to 110 rpm and "honking" out of the saddle in a big gear. Each can be accomplished by simply changing gears. In fact, during bad weather, you can practice them on an indoor resistance trainer.   *Christine L. Wells, Ph.D.*

Pack Makes Her Panic

For some reason, whenever I ride with more than two cyclists, I get nervous. Do you have any suggestions for overcoming this fear?   Maria Musciano, Somerdale, N.J.

To ride in traffic, whether it be among motorists or other cyclists, you must be relaxed, confident, and in control of your bike. If you have a tense upper body and a death grip on the handlebar, you'll be unable to ride a straight line. Chances are, you'll wobble and zigzag your way into trouble. So, relax. Keep your elbows unlocked and your grip only moderately tight. If you begin to get nervous, take a few deep breaths. How much control you have over your bike also depends on how well it fits. So have this checked at a bike shop (or consult the sections on bike fit in this book). The more often you ride with a group, the less nervous you'll feel. Join a touring club and attend its weekend group rides. Practice your paceline riding with those who seem the smoothest. Start by staying one bike length from the rider in front, then gradually close the gap as you become more confident of your abilities. Watch the road past the rider's shoulder or leg, rather than staring at the wheel. In time, you should be riding within a wheel's length— and enjoying the effects of drafting.   *John Kukoda*

Staying Hydrated

How much should I drink during a ride? Is it possible to drink too much?   John Rutledge, El Cajon, Calif.

The amount and type of solution a rider should drink depends on two factors: (1) the need to offset dehydration, and (2) the need to supplement the body's limited store of carbohydrates. Two water bottles per hour (one bottle = 20 ounces or 600 ml) is about as much as most people can tolerate, but everyone must experiment to find his or her limit. A general recommendation is to drink 6 to 12 ounces every 15 to 30 minutes. Although there have been rare reports of endurance athletes diluting their vital body fluids by drinking large amounts of water, generally the only risk in drinking too much is feeling bloated or sick.

For rides less than 2 hours, water is all you need. On warm days when you sweat more, drink as much as possible. The less dehydrated your body becomes, the less fatigued you'll feel. Also remember that a cool drink is not only more refreshing, but empties from the stomach into the bloodstream faster.

For rides longer than 2 hours, it's best to drink solutions containing sugar or starch. These delay fatigue by keeping the body's store of carbohydrates high. Commercial energy or sports drinks, for instance, contain 6 to 10 percent carbohydrate. This is present in the form of glucose, glucose polymers (starches), or table sugar (sucrose). Fruit juices, which contain fruit sugar or fructose, are not as effective because they don't convert as quickly into energy.

Since it takes time for carbohydrate solutions to work, you should begin drinking 30 to 60 minutes into a long ride. These mixtures also empty more slowly from the stomach, so the total amount ingested should be reduced by 5 to 10 ounces every 15 to 30 minutes. Table 4-1 lists a few popular energy drinks and their carbohydrate concentration. Do some experimenting to find one that suits your tastes and needs.

TABLE 4-1.
Energy Drinks

Name	Carbohydrate (%)	Type of Carbohydrate
Recharge	7.6	Fructose, glucose
Max	7.5	Glucose polymers, fructose
Exceed	7.0	Glucose polymers, fructose
Isostar	7.0	Sucrose, glucose, fructose
Gatorade	6.0	Sucrose, glucose
Gookinaid E.R.G.	5.0	Glucose
BodyFuel	4.5	Glucose polymers

Chairman of the Bored

I'm a 19-year-old male with a problem. When I ride I get bored after approximately 25 miles. In fact, I find myself not wanting to cycle because of it. Please help me.   Mark Beaupre, Tucson, Ariz.

First, vary your route. This will transform tedious rides into new visual experiences. Then, turn your casual outings into training rides by adding a series of intervals. Sprint for traffic signs, attack the hills, or pretend you're in a race. This, too, will break the monotony.

Another solution may be to join a local cycling club. Organized tours or training rides with other cyclists are usually more exciting than going alone. Plus, you'll learn about different training techniques and equipment that will contribute to your overall progress. One note of caution, though: In your battle against boredom, avoid wearing stereo headphones. There have been too many accidents involving cyclists who were tuned out of their environment.   *Edmund R. Burke, Ph.D.*

Sleeping Toes

My toes fall asleep about 2 hours into a ride. I've changed shoes, but the problem persists. What should I do?   Tony De Almeida, Pasadena, Calif.

Loosen your shoes. It's that simple, yet it didn't dawn on me during years of riding with toes that tingled, burned, throbbed, and eventually went numb. I even squirted water into my shoes to put out the "fire." The problem is actually caused when feet swell during a ride, eventually making shoes too tight. This puts pressure on nerves and reduces blood circulation, which creates the discomforts that result in numbness. My feet are as accurate as an odometer. By 70 miles, they're uncomfortable enough to make me stop and loosen the laces. *John Kukoda*

Out of Shape

I'm approximately 50 pounds overweight and haven't been on a bike since I was a child. I'd like to start cycling for fitness and pleasure, but I have no idea where to begin. What do you suggest for a terribly out-of-shape 30-year-old woman?   M. M., Enterprise, Ala.

Start by adopting a high-carbohydrate, low-fat diet. Omit fried foods and baked goods, add lots of fresh fruits and vegetables, and eat red meat sparingly. For further advice consult an experienced dietitian in your area.

Regarding a training program, I suggest easy riding in a low gear. Make cycling 10 miles in 1 hour your goal, and then gradually increase your speed and distance (about 2 miles at a time) as you become fit. Two common mistakes made by beginners are trying to keep pace with more accomplished riders and pedaling in a gear that's too high. To avoid these pitfalls, do your own thing at your own speed. Ride about three or four times a week. Stick with this program and results will follow.   *Christine L. Wells, Ph.D.*

Beginning Racer

I'm a 16-year-old girl who's been cycling for four years and average 10 mph on my usual rides. I would like to get into competitive racing, but there's hardly any news about it where I live. How can I find out about races in my area, and how should I prepare for them? Does it take a certain number of years of experience? Also, I want to buy a racing bike. Would it be smart to invest in an expensive brand?   Linda Wu, Browns Mills, N.J.

In order to compete in sanctioned bicycle racing, you'll have to obtain a license from the U.S. Cycling Federation (USCF), 1750 E. Boulder St., Colorado Springs, CO 80909. In addition, I suggest you visit a local bicycle shop and ask about clubs in the area involved with developmental racing. You and your parents will need advice on types of racing, equipment, and training, and shops and clubs can be excellent resources. If you have trouble locating a good club in your area, contact the USCF. It can put you in touch with its New Jersey representative, who can direct you to one.

I suggest your first bicycle be moderately priced since, at your age, you will most likely outgrow it. Once you've met some cyclists and raced a few times, you'll have a better idea of how to upgrade your equipment. You're lucky in that you've discovered cycling at a young age. You can look forward to many years of improvement and enjoyment.
Edmund R. Burke, Ph.D.

Starting Out

I'm 15 years old and recently became very interested in racing. The salesman at my local shop helped me choose the right bike, but I need training advice. Can you help me?   Julie Smith, Burke, Va.

First, master the basics of proper technique. Learn to ride a straight line and concentrate on pedaling or "spinning" at a high cadence (90 to 110 revolutions per minute).

Next, build your mileage base. Start the season slowly with a few short rides to gain fitness. When you're able to ride four or more times a week, gradually increase the distance of your long ride to at least twice the mileage of your regular training rides (i.e., if you ride 15 miles on weekdays, try going 30 on Saturday or Sunday).

After you've built a solid base (about a third of your estimated yearly mileage), incorporate some hillwork or interval training into your schedule once or twice a week. Find a hill you can climb without exhausting yourself. After a sufficient warm-up, climb it, recover on the way down, and then go up again. As your fitness improves, add more repeats.

Intervals develop speed. They can range from structured ¼-, ½-, or 1-mile repeats to random sprints between telephone poles along a fairly flat road. Again, begin with an easy warm-up and gradually increase the number of sprints. End each session with an easy ride home. By following these suggestions, you'll be logging quality miles that promote power, speed, and endurance.   *Kate Delhagen*

The Perfect Pulse

When I started cycling a year ago, my resting pulse rate was 78 to 82 beats per minute (bpm). Now it's 48 to 50 bpm. I'm a 6-foot, 152-pound male who rides a hilly 9-mile course three to four times per week. How much lower can I expect my heart rate to fall? How low is safe?   David Fasig, Middletown, Pa.

A low heart rate due to athletic conditioning is never unsafe. In fact, some well-trained athletes have resting heart rates under

40. As you've experienced, training can cause a substantial decline in resting heart rate. With a more rigorous riding schedule, I suspect yours will fall to 45.   *David L. Smith, M.D.*

Car Fumes

I ride a lot in the city and am concerned about having to breathe the auto and truck exhaust. Have there been any studies done on its effect on cyclists? Can it be compared to breathing secondhand cigarette smoke? Would wearing a painter's mask protect me from it?   Matthew Lombard, Norfolk, Va.

There have been studies on the effects of air pollution on cyclists. Some have shown adverse short-term effects on the lungs. But, to my knowledge, no study has shown adverse long-term effects such as emphysema or lung cancer. An interesting study a few years ago, however, did find that children living near busy highways had higher levels of lead in their systems, presumably due to the exhaust from vehicles using leaded gasoline. Nevertheless, air pollution is definitely not as dangerous as breathing secondhand tobacco smoke, which can cause emphysema and lung cancer.

A painter's mask won't protect you from air pollution, but a device called a respirator will. The civilian equivalent of a gas mask, it filters many toxins from the air. In any case, though, riding in a polluted environment is still better than not riding at all.   *David L. Smith, M.D.*

Upper-Body Power

What weight exercises can I do to increase the strength and endurance of my legs and upper body for cycling?
Jim Bolich, Milton, Pa.

If you want to lift weights, your best bet is to visit a health club or other training facility and have a professional devise a custom program. Choose the gym carefully by checking the qualifications of the staff. Be aware that weight training for strength is different than weight training for endurance, so you need to clarify your objectives. Basically, to build strength you should do fewer repetitions with heavier weights. Conversely, to build muscular endurance do more repetitions with lighter weights.

You can also increase upper-body strength at home by using your own body weight as resistance. The best exercises are push-ups, pull-ups, and tricep dips (get between two tables or chairs, place a hand on each, and slowly lower and raise yourself). To build midbody strength, which will help maintain a good riding position, do a few sets of abdominal crunches (lie on your back with your lower legs on a bench or bed, curl your head and shoulders off the floor, reach your hands past your knees and hold for 3 to 5 seconds) and back extensions (lying on your stomach with your hands on your buttocks, slowly lift your head and shoulders from the floor and hold for 3 to 5 seconds. Repeat 10 to 20 times).
Christine L. Wells, Ph.D.

Genital Numbness

I'm a 31-year-old male who has been experiencing genital numbness during my daily rides. Is this a common problem? Will it cause permanent damage? How can I remedy it?
T. S., Spotswood, N.J.

Genital numbness is a common problem resulting from pressure on the nerves leading to the penis or on the blood vessels feeding these nerves. Theoretically, if you ride all day in a numb condition, the nerves could be damaged and take several weeks or months to recover. This would inhibit sexual performance, but you would not be rendered infertile. Although I've received many letters from riders who have experienced prolonged hand numbness, I've not heard of extended genital numbness.

To remedy your condition, try raising or lowering your saddle slightly, or angling its nose down a bit. It's important that your weight be borne by the hind portion of the saddle where your sit bones rest, rather than the front end that

contacts the nerves and other soft tissues. You may need a saddle that's wider in the rear and/or narrower in front.
David L. Smith, M.D.

Heart Monitors

Help! I'm swamped with information on heart monitors. How important are these gadgets to someone just starting out? How accurate are they? What's the difference between a heart monitor and a pulse monitor?   Venu Rao, Austin, Tex.

A heart or pulse monitor (they're the same thing) can be a valuable training device. But it's just a tool and it won't automatically make you a better cyclist. Through systematic use, however, it will enable you to progress more rapidly to a higher fitness level.

Such monitors supply mechanical feedback about your heart rate during training. This is especially valuable when you're trying to train within a specific pulse range in order to accomplish a desired effect. Heart monitors will help you stay there and prevent you from overextending yourself.

Because they detect the weak electrical activity of the heart muscle, the most accurate monitors use a chest belt with electrode pads to detect heartbeat. A transmitter amplifies the heart's electrical current and sends it to the monitor either by wire or wireless telemetry. Earlobe or fingertip sensors are less accurate at higher heart rates.

Several studies have compared readings from chest-mount monitors with those from an EKG machine. They were found equally suitable for measuring heart rate during exercise and for analyzing training intensity.   *Edmund R. Burke, Ph.D.*

Pre-Event Insomnia

Why can't I ever get a good night's sleep before a big ride?
Stephen E. Halton, Carmichael, Calif.

Athletes often have difficulty getting a good night's sleep

before a major event. The reasons range from anxiety to excitement.

I suggest you integrate a relaxation exercise into your preride schedule. A typical exercise usually takes about 20 minutes. Start by lying on your bed and taking long, deep breaths. Count slowly from one to five and close your eyes. Next, tighten and loosen each muscle group from your head to your toes. Begin with your forehead and proceed to your jaw, neck, shoulders, arms, stomach, buttocks, thighs, calves, and feet. Flex and relax each muscle group twice.

By this time, you should feel physically relaxed. Next, visualize yourself in a peaceful environment such as the beach or the mountains. Let yourself absorb the positive scenery. This should allow you to drift off to sleep. If you have trouble doing this on your own, audio relaxation tapes might help. *Andrew Jacobs, Ph.D.*

Improving Speed

When I finish a ride and check my cyclecomputer, I always seem to average 15 mph no matter what the distance. When I ride with others and they decide to sprint, I'm left in the dust. My endurance is fine, but how can I improve my speed?
Carol Jones, Baltimore, Md.

Many new riders adopt a favorite gear and train their bodies to pedal at precisely that pace. When the time comes to ride faster, their muscles don't know how to respond.

Fortunately, muscles are excellent students. You can train them to unleash 25 mph (or faster) bursts on your unsuspecting friends. Here's how: In the spring, after you establish a substantial mileage base, add a weekly hill workout. Start slowly. Become familiar with the intensity changes that accompany climbing and descending. Then, when you feel comfortable, concentrate on working the hills—jam on the way up, recover on the descent. Do a few hard repeats while gradually increasing the intensity and distance of each workout.

After a few weeks, add a second hill workout or incorporate intervals into your weekly schedule. To do intervals, pick a time or distance within your regular training ride and cycle faster than average for that segment. For instance, try riding 18 mph for 5 minutes of your ride. Eventually, increase this to 10 minutes, then 15 minutes.

In addition, to build good early season power, find a mile-long stretch of road and ride as hard as you can for its entire length, then turn around and recover on the way back by spinning a low gear. Start with two or three repeats and build to ten over the course of six to eight weeks.

As an important ride draws near, shorten the distances of hill and interval repeats and increase speed. For instance, reduce the all-out one-mile stretches to a half mile. By then, when the time comes to sprint with your friends, your legs will know what to do.   *Kate Delhagen*

High Cholesterol

I'm a 41-year-old recreational rider. I just got a medical checkup and everything is fine except for my cholesterol count, which is 270. According to everything I've read, this means I have one foot in the grave. I'd like to get it out, but my job as a bike shop manager keeps me so busy that I eat a lot of junk food. My doctor says I should improve my diet and then get retested in a couple of months. Is there a magic way to reduce my cholesterol? What is an acceptable level for a cyclist my age?   Bob Hughes, Saint-Jean-sur-Richelieu, Quebec

There are two types of cholesterol—one positive, the other negative. High-density lipoprotein (HDL) cholesterol is good, low-density lipoprotein (LDL) cholesterol is bad. Ask your doctor to check the ratio between these two types. In determining your risk of heart attack, this ratio is more important than your overall cholesterol level.

As a cyclist, you may be pleasantly surprised by this ratio. Among those who exercise a great deal, a high overall count may be partly caused by an elevated level of good cholesterol. If this is true in your case, that 270 might not be as ominous as it seems.

Regardless of your ratio, though, you'll be better off with

an overall level below 200. One way to achieve this is by improving your diet. Much evidence has been published on the link between diet and heart disease. Ask your doctor for some dietary guidelines. One major tenet is avoiding saturated fat, which is abundant in junk food. High cholesterol is a serious problem requiring lifestyle changes. Cycling helps, but eating better helps even more.   *David L. Smith, M.D.*

Arm Discomfort

While touring I discovered that my arms became weak on long descents, making it difficult to grasp the handlebar. What can I do to prevent this?   Layn Leudtke, Portland, Oreg.

While descending, your weight shifts forward onto your arms. This problem is compounded by the aerodynamic "tuck" position used by many riders. To relieve tension in the arms and upper back, frequently change position. Move your hands from the handlebar drops to atop the brake hoods, and occasionally sit up. Pedaling also helps keep you supple. Keep turning the crank even when you're going too fast to engage the freewheel. But most important, relax. Don't lock your elbows or use a "death grip" on the bar. And unless you're racing, don't maintain an uncomfortable position just for aerodynamics.   *Steve Johnson, Ph.D.*

Quality Time

How do people with full schedules find time to train? My job keeps me behind a desk for at least 8 hours a day, and I take a college course two nights a week. My weekly riding consists of a 15- to 25-mile ride at a local track on Tuesday, and 20- to 40-mile road rides on Thursday and Saturday. I also lift weights on Friday and Sunday.   Peter C. Nowack, Jr., Greensboro, N.C.

When it comes to training, the important thing is quality, not quantity. Your 55- to 105-weekly miles are plenty to achieve excellent aerobic fitness, as long as you're riding intensely enough.

To gauge intensity, listen to your heart. Determining your optimum training heart rate is easy. First, subtract your age from 220. The result is an estimation of your maximum heart rate in beats per minute (bpm). Current research says that to benefit from aerobic activity, you need to exercise at 60 to 85 percent of your maximum heart rate and sustain it for more than 20 minutes. This range is known as your target heart rate zone. Yours is 114 to 162 bpm. When you ride, aim for the middle of this range, say 145 to 150 bpm. To check this, take your pulse periodically or wear a heart monitor.
Edmund R. Burke, Ph.D.

Running vs. Cycling

During the summer I race as a USCF junior, and in the fall I run for my high school cross-country team. I know that running keeps me in great shape, but I've heard it also builds muscles I'll never need for cycling. On the other hand, I know some top racers who cross-train by running. Will running help or hinder my bicycle racing?   David Kelly, Roseville, Calif.

Running, like cycling, is an excellent way to develop cardio-vascular fitness. But whether running will help your cycling is a controversial point among exercise physiologists, coaches, and athletes.

Some experts argue that any activity that builds aerobic fitness positively affects performance in other aerobic activities. Others argue that sport-specific training is the only way to improve.

As for muscular development, running primarily works the muscles along the back of the legs—the hamstrings and calves. Bicycling primarily works those along the front of the legs, especially the quadriceps or thigh muscles, in addition to the hip and buttock muscles. This is where one undisputed advantage of cross-training comes into play: By mixing running into your cycling program, you'll achieve better balance between opposing muscle groups, such as the hamstrings and quads, and protect yourself against injury.

If cycling is your primary sport, decrease your running

and increase your riding come spring. During summer, spend most of your time cycling, with only an occasional run (maybe on your days off the bike). In September and October, gear up again for the cross-country season and then use running as part of your winter training program.   *Kate Delhagen*

Leg Cramps

At the end of a recent long ride, I stood up to push hard and every leg muscle suddenly cramped. A friend suggested taking salt tablets, but I've heard they do more harm than good. What do you recommend?   Todd Ryan, Painesville, Ohio

Such cramping is due not to lack of salt but rather to lack of fuel. Muscles prefer to run on glycogen, the stored form of carbohydrates. When this fuel isn't present, muscles sometimes rebel by cramping. To prevent this, your diet should be rich in carbohydrates. Try eating pasta or rice before a big ride and nutritious snacks such as bananas or PowerBars while cycling. A sports drink also works well since it delivers carbohydrates in an easily digestible form.   *David L. Smith, M.D.*

Indoor vs. Outdoor

I'm curious if I get the same benefit using my bicycle on an indoor resistance trainer as I get when riding outside.
Thomas A. Harman, Wilmington, Del.

Riding an indoor resistance trainer is quite effective for conditioning your cardiovascular and muscular system. By training regularly at 60 to 75 percent of your maximum heart rate, you'll be able to maintain or improve your level of aerobic fitness, which is the ability to ride at low intensity for long periods.

However, anaerobic fitness—the ability to ride at high intensity for short periods—is more difficult to achieve. For this, you need dramatic increases in pedaling resistance, the kind you encounter when attacking a short hill. To duplicate this it helps to have an indoor trainer with adjustable resistance setting. Increasing the resistance encourages you to get out of the saddle and work hard, just as you would on the road.

As far as conditioning your muscles, there's little difference between riding indoors or out. This is because you're using the same bike, the same pedaling motion and, therefore, the same muscles.   *Steve Johnson, Ph.D.*

23 WHERE TO GO FOR MORE INFORMATION

We've told you how to choose a bicycle, briefed you on the basic rules of the road, and given you training tips for a variety of events. Now you know everything about the sport. Well, not quite. The following is a list of groups, organizations, and associations that cater to cyclists. They can help you explore a particular area of interest or answer your questions about specific events or programs. Also, be sure to attend a meeting of the nearest bike club, which is the best way to meet cyclists and learn about local activities.

American Youth Hostels (AYH)
Box 37613
Washington, DC 20013-7613
(202) 783-6161

AYH is a national, nonprofit organization that provides touring cyclists with inexpensive accommodations—ranging from converted hotels to former lighthouses—throughout the world. There are more than 5,000 hostels in 74 countries. AYH also conducts a variety of bicycle tours in North America, Europe, and New Zealand. Membership is $20 for 18- to 54-year-olds and $10 if you're under 17 or over 55.

Bikecentennial
Box 8308
Missoula, MT 59807
(406) 721-1776

The largest recreational cycling organization in the country, Bikecentennial sells maps of the 15,000 miles of roads it has linked into low-traffic, scenic cycling routes. An individual membership is $22, and family memberships are $25. Membership includes a copy of "The Cyclist's Yellow Pages," a comprehensive guide to bicycle trip planning.

Canadian Cycling Association (CCA)
1600 James Naismith Dr.
Gloucester, Ontario, K1B 5N4
(613) 748-5629

The CCA is the governing body for amateur and professional cycling in Canada. It can answer questions about racing rules and regulations. It's also the place to go for information on touring, safety, and other recreational cycling concerns. The CCA has a number of maps and publications.

Collegiate Cycling
Kathy Volski
11300 Regency Green Dr.
Cypress, TX 77429

Kathy Volski is the U.S. Cycling Federation's liaison for information on collegiate cycling in the United States. She can help you start a cycling club at your school or direct you to a competitive conference in your area.

International Human-Powered Vehicle Association
Box 51255
Indianapolis, IN 46251-0255
(317) 876-9478

A nonprofit organization dedicated to promoting improvement, innovation, and creativity in the design and development of human-powered vehicles. It sponsors an annual competition for such vehicles.

League of American Wheelmen (LAW)
Suite 209
6706 Whitestone Rd.
Baltimore, MD 21207
(301) 944-3399

LAW protects the rights and promotes the interests of cyclists. It can answer questions about new or existing bicycle clubs and help you fight anti-bike legislation in your area. LAW serves a nationwide network of affiliated cycling clubs and sponsors bicycle rallies, centuries, and other cycling-related activities.

Ultra Marathon Cycling Association (UMCA)
4790 Irvine Blvd.
Irvine, CA 92720
(714) 544-1701

The UMCA is a clearinghouse for information about ultra-endurance cycling. It organizes the Race Across America (RAAM) and a National Points Challenge program that offers recognition and awards for cyclists completing the most long-distance events in one year.

U.S. Cycling Federation (USCF)
1750 East Boulder St.
Colorado Springs, CO 80909
(719) 578-4581

The governing body for U.S. amateur road, off-road, and track racing, the USCF can provide you with all the necessary information to get started. Before you can participate in a USCF-sanctioned race you must be licensed. Applications are available at most bicycle shops or by writing the USCF. The cost is $32 per year.

Women's Cycling Network (WCN)
Box 73
Harvard, IL 60033

Through all-women seminars, rides, and workshops, the WCN helps female cyclists achieve their personal goals, as well as share cycling information and experiences. A list of events is published in the *Women's Cycling News,* a quarterly newsletter. The WCN also publishes a national directory, which lists "hospitality homes" where women can stay when touring. Individual memberships are $10 and club memberships cost $30.

◼ CREDITS

The information in this book was drawn from these and other articles in *Bicycling* magazine.

"Choosing the Right Bike" John Kukoda, "How to Choose the Right Bike," February 1989; Fred Zahradnik, "Overview of Racing, Sport/Touring, Mountain, and Women's Models," March 1989.

"Questions to Ask Before You Buy" John Kukoda, "Questions to Ask Before You Buy," February 1989.

"Sizing a New Bike" Frank Berto, "Sizing a New Bike," March 1987.

"Clothing and Accessory Checklist" Fred Zahradnik, "Clothing and Accessory Checklist," February 1989.

"The Principles of Pedaling" Susan Sorensen, "The Principles of Pedaling," February 1989.

"Learning the Lingo" Nelson Pena, "Learning the Lingo," August 1987.

"Your First Riding Lesson" Scott Martin, "Your First Riding Lesson," February 1989.

"Sharing the Road" James Hargett, "Keeping Drivers Friendly," August 1989.

"How to Out-Psych Hostile Drivers" Gary Stanton, "One for the Rogue," July 1987.

"The Facts about Cycling Nutrition" Susan Sorensen, "The Facts about Cycling Nutrition," February 1989.

"Fast Foods" Ellen Coleman, "Twinkie Power," August 1989.

"Perfect Your Riding Position" John Kukoda, "Sitting Pretty," April 1987.

"Smart Shifting" Frank Berto, "Smart Shifting," April 1989.

"Basic Bike Care" Jim Langley, "Basic Bike Care," February 1989.

"Fixing a Flat" Don Cuerdon, "Clincher Tire Repair," April 1988.

"Setting Goals" Nelson Pena, "Rip Out This Page," March 1988.

"Training for an Extended Tour" John Kukoda, "Get Ready to Ride," April 1987.

"Preparing for a Century" Scott Martin, "Century Ride Training Guide," August 1988.

"Becoming a Racer" Fred Matheny, "New Racer," March 1989.

"What Ails You?" Edmund R. Burke, Ph.D., "What Ails You?" April 1989.

"75 Tips for Shaping Up, Losing Weight and Riding Better," Geoff Drake and the Bicycling staff, April 1990.

"Questions and Answers" "Fitness Q&A," various issues.

"Where to Go for More Information" Susan Sorensen, "Where to Go for More Information," February 1989.

Photographs and Illustrations

John P. Hamel: photo 1-1; Rodale Stock Images: photos 2-1, 2-2, 2-3.

Catherine L. Reed: illustrations 1-1, 1-2; Sally Onopa: illustrations 2-1, 2-4, 2-5.

Rodale Press, Inc., publishes BICYCLING, America's leading cycling magazine. For information on how to order your subscription, write to BICYCLING, Emmaus, PA 18098.